# little book
## of **MISSING**
# MONEY

---

**A Quick and Easy Guide
to Finding Money
that is Rightfully Yours**

---

**FOURTH EDITION**

**MARY PITMAN**

Fourth Edition

© Copyright 2019.

ISBN#: 978-0-9911936-1-5

Do the Right Thing Publishing

# Welcome!

I know you want to get right into how to search for and find money on unclaimed.org and the other sites I recommend.

Good luck on your treasure hunt! Post your success stories on the Missing Money Book page on Facebook. Inspire others!

## Keep up with the latest developments

Follow me on Twitter @MaryFindsMoney for updates as they become available.

"Like" MissingMoneyBook on Facebook, where I post information about deadlines for filing and other missing money tidbits.

# Contents

Success Stories . . . . . . . . . . . . . . . . . . . . . . . . . . . . . xi
Foreword . . . . . . . . . . . . . . . . . . . . . . . . . . . . . . . . . xv
Preface . . . . . . . . . . . . . . . . . . . . . . . . . . . . . . . . . . xvii
Introduction . . . . . . . . . . . . . . . . . . . . . . . . . . . . . . . 1
The Terminology . . . . . . . . . . . . . . . . . . . . . . . . . . . . 3
Finder's Fees—to pay or not to pay . . . . . . . . . . . . . . . 5
Avoid Missing Money Scams . . . . . . . . . . . . . . . . . . . . 13
Legitimate notices . . . . . . . . . . . . . . . . . . . . . . . . . . . 15
What's New? . . . . . . . . . . . . . . . . . . . . . . . . . . . . . . . 17

75 SEARCH TIPS . . . . . . . . . . . . . . . . . . . . . . . . . . . . 23
    The Basics . . . . . . . . . . . . . . . . . . . . . . . . . . . . . . . 23
    The Name Game . . . . . . . . . . . . . . . . . . . . . . . . . . . 27
CHARITIES AND CHURCHES . . . . . . . . . . . . . . . . . . . . 35
HOSPITALS . . . . . . . . . . . . . . . . . . . . . . . . . . . . . . . . 37
BUSINESSES AND CORPORATIONS . . . . . . . . . . . . . . . 39
LOCAL, STATE AND FEDERAL . . . . . . . . . . . . . . . . . . . 43

108 PLACES TO LOOK
THE GOVERNMENT . . . . . . . . . . . . . . . . . . . . . . . . . . 47
    Social Security Administration . . . . . . . . . . . . . . . . . 47
    Savings Bonds . . . . . . . . . . . . . . . . . . . . . . . . . . . . 48
    Workers Owed Wages . . . . . . . . . . . . . . . . . . . . . . . 51
    Veterans Administration . . . . . . . . . . . . . . . . . . . . . 52
    Financial Management Services . . . . . . . . . . . . . . . . 54
    IRS . . . . . . . . . . . . . . . . . . . . . . . . . . . . . . . . . . . . 56

COURTS . . . . . . . . . . . . . . . . . . . . . . . . . . . . . . . . . . 57
    Court Registry . . . . . . . . . . . . . . . . . . . . . . . . . . . . 57
    Unclaimed Criminal Restitution . . . . . . . . . . . . . . . 58
    U.S. Bankruptcy Court . . . . . . . . . . . . . . . . . . . . . . 59
    Canadian Bankruptcy . . . . . . . . . . . . . . . . . . . . . . 60
    Class Action Lawsuits . . . . . . . . . . . . . . . . . . . . . . . 60

Child Support Payments . . . . . . . . . . . . . . . . . . . 61
Illinois—Cook County . . . . . . . . . . . . . . . . . . . . . 63
Ohio—Franklin County . . . . . . . . . . . . . . . . . . . . 63
Ohio—Summit County . . . . . . . . . . . . . . . . . . . . 63
Oregon. . . . . . . . . . . . . . . . . . . . . . . . . . . . . . . . 63
South Carolina. . . . . . . . . . . . . . . . . . . . . . . . . . 63
Wisconsin . . . . . . . . . . . . . . . . . . . . . . . . . . . . . 64

**BANKING, FINANCIAL SERVICES, STOCKS** . . . . . . . . . . 65
Stocks. . . . . . . . . . . . . . . . . . . . . . . . . . . . . . . . 65
Investors Claims Funds . . . . . . . . . . . . . . . . . . . 68
NCUA . . . . . . . . . . . . . . . . . . . . . . . . . . . . . . . . 69
FDIC . . . . . . . . . . . . . . . . . . . . . . . . . . . . . . . . . 70
HUD/FHA Refunds. . . . . . . . . . . . . . . . . . . . . . . 71
Safe Deposit Boxes . . . . . . . . . . . . . . . . . . . . . . 73

**PERFORMANCE ROYALTIES**. . . . . . . . . . . . . . . . . . . . 75
**Preventing Lost Royalty Payments** . . . . . . . . . . . . 76
**Music Publishing** . . . . . . . . . . . . . . . . . . . . . . . . . 78
EMI. . . . . . . . . . . . . . . . . . . . . . . . . . . . . . . . . . 78
Sony . . . . . . . . . . . . . . . . . . . . . . . . . . . . . . . . . 78
Universal . . . . . . . . . . . . . . . . . . . . . . . . . . . . . . 78
Warner Music Group. . . . . . . . . . . . . . . . . . . . . 78

**Professional Organizations/Union** . . . . . . . . . . . . 79
AARC . . . . . . . . . . . . . . . . . . . . . . . . . . . . . . . . 79
SAG/AFTRA . . . . . . . . . . . . . . . . . . . . . . . . . . . 79
APRA . . . . . . . . . . . . . . . . . . . . . . . . . . . . . . . . 79
Director's Guild of America . . . . . . . . . . . . . . . 80
Writer's Guild of America. . . . . . . . . . . . . . . . . 80
Recording Artists Royalties. . . . . . . . . . . . . . . . 81

**Performing Rights Organizations** . . . . . . . . . . . . . 81
ASCAP . . . . . . . . . . . . . . . . . . . . . . . . . . . . . . . 81
Broadcast Music, Inc.. . . . . . . . . . . . . . . . . . . . . 81
SESAC. . . . . . . . . . . . . . . . . . . . . . . . . . . . . . . . 82
Sound Exchange . . . . . . . . . . . . . . . . . . . . . . . . 82

**RETIREMENT BENEFITS –**

Contributed by Peter Preovolos . . . . . . . . . . . . . . . . . . . . 85
    Uncashed/Stale-dated checks . . . . . . . . . . . . . . . . . . 85
    Terminated 401K Plans . . . . . . . . . . . . . . . . . . . . . 90
    NRURB . . . . . . . . . . . . . . . . . . . . . . . . . . . . . . 92
    PBGC. . . . . . . . . . . . . . . . . . . . . . . . . . . . . . . 93
    Thrift Savings Plans . . . . . . . . . . . . . . . . . . . . . . . 94
    Federal Employees/Civil Service . . . . . . . . . . . . . . . 94
    U.S. Railroad Retirement Board . . . . . . . . . . . . . . . 95
    NY State Deferred Compensation . . . . . . . . . . . . . 95
    SC Retirement System . . . . . . . . . . . . . . . . . . . . . 95
    WI State Retirement . . . . . . . . . . . . . . . . . . . . . . 96
    Other State Retirement Programs . . . . . . . . . . . . . 96

**LIFE INSURANCE (U.S. and Canada)** . . . . . . . . . . . . . . . 97
    American Council of Life Insurers . . . . . . . . . . . . 100
    New York Life Unclaimed Assets . . . . . . . . . . . . . 101
    John Hancock . . . . . . . . . . . . . . . . . . . . . . . . . 101
    Met Life . . . . . . . . . . . . . . . . . . . . . . . . . . . . . 101
    Veterans Life Insurance. . . . . . . . . . . . . . . . . . . . 101
    Survivor Benefits . . . . . . . . . . . . . . . . . . . . . . . . 103
    FERS Death Benefits . . . . . . . . . . . . . . . . . . . . . 103
    The State of New York . . . . . . . . . . . . . . . . . . . . 105
    Ohio Department of Insurance . . . . . . . . . . . . . . 105
    Louisiana Dept. of Insurance . . . . . . . . . . . . . . . 106
    NAIC. . . . . . . . . . . . . . . . . . . . . . . . . . . . . . . 107
    MIB . . . . . . . . . . . . . . . . . . . . . . . . . . . . . . . . 107
    Lost Life Insurance Finder Expert . . . . . . . . . . . . 107
    FindYourPolicy.com . . . . . . . . . . . . . . . . . . . . . 108
    Canada Life/Great-West Life. . . . . . . . . . . . . . . . 108
    Sun Life Canada. . . . . . . . . . . . . . . . . . . . . . . . 108

**INTERNATIONAL UNCLAIMED PROPERTY** . . . . . . . . . 109
**Canada** . . . . . . . . . . . . . . . . . . . . . . . . . . . . . . . . . . 109
    Bank of Canada. . . . . . . . . . . . . . . . . . . . . . . . . 109
    British Columbia . . . . . . . . . . . . . . . . . . . . . . . . 109
    Quebec. . . . . . . . . . . . . . . . . . . . . . . . . . . . . . 110

Alberta. . . . . . . . . . . . . . . . . . . . . . . . . . . . . . . . . . . . 110
NS Intestate Unclaimed Funds . . . . . . . . . . . . . . . 110
NS Credit Union. . . . . . . . . . . . . . . . . . . . . . . . . . . 110
Bankruptcy Court of Canada . . . . . . . . . . . . . . . . 111

**United Kingdom** . . . . . . . . . . . . . . . . . . . . . . . . . . . . 111
  **England**. . . . . . . . . . . . . . . . . . . . . . . . . . . . . . . . . 111
    Child Trust Funds. . . . . . . . . . . . . . . . . . . . . . . . 111
    Bona Vacantia . . . . . . . . . . . . . . . . . . . . . . . . . . 112
    Pension Tracking Service. . . . . . . . . . . . . . . . . . 112
    Unclaimed Assets Register . . . . . . . . . . . . . . . . 112
  **Scotland** . . . . . . . . . . . . . . . . . . . . . . . . . . . . . . . 112
    Citizens Advice . . . . . . . . . . . . . . . . . . . . . . . . . 112
  **Ireland**. . . . . . . . . . . . . . . . . . . . . . . . . . . . . . . . . 113

**Europe** . . . . . . . . . . . . . . . . . . . . . . . . . . . . . . . . . . . 113
  France. . . . . . . . . . . . . . . . . . . . . . . . . . . . . . . . . . . 113
  Switzerland. . . . . . . . . . . . . . . . . . . . . . . . . . . . . . 113
  Greece. . . . . . . . . . . . . . . . . . . . . . . . . . . . . . . . . . . 113

**Australia** . . . . . . . . . . . . . . . . . . . . . . . . . . . . . . . . . 114
  ASIC. . . . . . . . . . . . . . . . . . . . . . . . . . . . . . . . . . . . 114
  Australian Tax Office . . . . . . . . . . . . . . . . . . . . . . 114
  New Zealand. . . . . . . . . . . . . . . . . . . . . . . . . . . . . 114

**Africa** . . . . . . . . . . . . . . . . . . . . . . . . . . . . . . . . . . . 114
  Kenya . . . . . . . . . . . . . . . . . . . . . . . . . . . . . . . . . . 114
  Uganda. . . . . . . . . . . . . . . . . . . . . . . . . . . . . . . . . 114

**Caribbean** . . . . . . . . . . . . . . . . . . . . . . . . . . . . . . . 115
  Jamaica. . . . . . . . . . . . . . . . . . . . . . . . . . . . . . . . . 115
  Cayman Islands. . . . . . . . . . . . . . . . . . . . . . . . . . 115
  Eastern Caribbean . . . . . . . . . . . . . . . . . . . . . . . 115

**Asia** . . . . . . . . . . . . . . . . . . . . . . . . . . . . . . . . . . . . . 116
  Israel . . . . . . . . . . . . . . . . . . . . . . . . . . . . . . . . . . . 116
  Malaysia . . . . . . . . . . . . . . . . . . . . . . . . . . . . . . . . 116
  India . . . . . . . . . . . . . . . . . . . . . . . . . . . . . . . . . . . 116
  Japan. . . . . . . . . . . . . . . . . . . . . . . . . . . . . . . . . . . 116

**COMPENSATION FUNDS** . . . . . . . . . . . . . . . . . . . . . . . 117
   9/11 Victim Compensation Fund . . . . . . . . . . . . 117
   RECA. . . . . . . . . . . . . . . . . . . . . . . . . . . . . . . . . . 117
   Holocaust Survivors. . . . . . . . . . . . . . . . . . . . . . . . 119
   Vaccine Injury Compensation Act. . . . . . . . . . . . 122
   Disaster Money . . . . . . . . . . . . . . . . . . . . . . . . . . 122
   Victims of Violent Crimes . . . . . . . . . . . . . . . . . . 122
   Airline Compensation . . . . . . . . . . . . . . . . . . . . . 123

**MISCELLANEOUS MONEY** . . . . . . . . . . . . . . . . . . . . 125
   Gift Cards. . . . . . . . . . . . . . . . . . . . . . . . . . . . . . . 125
   Escheat Estates . . . . . . . . . . . . . . . . . . . . . . . . . . 127
   Lawyer Trust Accounts . . . . . . . . . . . . . . . . . . . . 128
   Unpaid Foreign Claims . . . . . . . . . . . . . . . . . . . . 129
   Oil and Mineral Royalties . . . . . . . . . . . . . . . . . . 131
   Old Stock Certificates . . . . . . . . . . . . . . . . . . . . . 133
   Postal Money Orders. . . . . . . . . . . . . . . . . . . . . . 134
   Lost Luggage. . . . . . . . . . . . . . . . . . . . . . . . . . . . 134
   Recovered Stolen Property. . . . . . . . . . . . . . . . . . 135

**20 TIPS TO PREVENT YOUR MONEY
FROM GOING TO THE STATE** . . . . . . . . . . . . . . . . . . . 137

**CHANGE OF NAME/ADDRESS OR
EXECUTOR OF A WILL CHECKLIST** . . . . . . . . . . . . . . 145

**STATE UNCLAIMED PROPERTY CONTACTS** . . . . . . . . 153
   States . . . . . . . . . . . . . . . . . . . . . . . . . . . . . . . . . 154
   U.S. Territories. . . . . . . . . . . . . . . . . . . . . . . . . . . 180
   Canada. . . . . . . . . . . . . . . . . . . . . . . . . . . . . . . . 181

**AFTERWORD** . . . . . . . . . . . . . . . . . . . . . . . . . . . . . . 183

**CONTACT MARY PITMAN/BULK SALES** . . . . . . . . . . . 185

# Success Stories

**Antoinette Furst**, San Diego, CA – "I'm an MBA who has always been meticulous with my finances. So when I heard from Mary that I had over $1100 in unclaimed funds with the state, I definitely didn't believe it. After a little research on my own, I came to find that Mary had uncovered money that was indeed mine that for sure would have been lost forever had she not contacted me. Mary's search tactics and knowledge of where to uncover lost money and how to do it is uncanny and hands down unlike anyone that exists today."

**Kathie Nelson**, Beaverton, OR – "Mary Pitman is a rock star. I don't know exactly how Mary does it but she is able to find money like no one I've ever seen!"

**Stephanie Miles,** East Saint Louis, MO – "I am elated and grateful to have found $1,300 in my dad's name. This money will be useful in providing homecare for my elderly mom."

**Annemarie Schuetz** – "My mother-in-law died so fast she had no time to get records in order. My sister-in-law and I are SURE that there is more money out there. Now we can find it – without hiring anyone. Thank you for this. What a difference you must be making for people."

**Germaine Leonard,** FL – "I found $646 from an insurance policy my parents bought when I was young. My sister found the money for me by going to Michigan's State Treasury. All I had to do was claim it. Thank you, Mary, for letting people know the possibilities."

**George Maher**, Vero Beach, FL – "Just got in and found an e-mail from a friend who listened to Mary on my broadcast yesterday. She followed Mary's simple instructions and found money within 3 minutes of beginning her search! This works!!!"

**Cina Wong**, Handwriting expert, Norfolk, VA – "Thanks to Mary Pitman I found approximately $144 the first time. Then last year, I decided to check again and found another $80. With what I learned, I found $14,000 for a friend!"

**Steve Olsher**, Author, *What is Your What?,* San Diego, CA – "Mary helped me save over $3,000 in finder's fees by showing me exactly what to do to claim $10,000+ owed to one of my companies. Everyone should read this book!!

**BullDog**, Radio Personality, WOCM – "One of the most eye-opening books I've read in years. Mary makes it easy to understand and I recovered almost $2,000!"

**Hank Guarenti**, Fullerton, CA – "I had never even heard of missing money until Mary told me she found $1440.56 for me. I received the refund in less than four weeks. Thank you, Mary!"

**Christopher M. Dermody, DMD**, Vero Beach, FL, found his money using search tip # 17 from the book and said, "Getting this money was easier than pulling a tooth with bone loss."

*Mary's note: Since the last edition, I found $504,500 in savings bonds left to a woman by her deceased dad. She did not want to be quoted, even anonymously. But finding more than half a million dollars for one person deserves being mentioned.*

# Foreword

The expression "Money makes the world go 'round" may be true, but some of it seems to get lost along the way. The whereabouts of some financial accounts goes astray, as do our car keys. Sometimes lost monies are held by companies or institutions we don't know about or have long forgotten; and just as importantly, they don't know us.

Mary Pitman has made an extraordinary effort to help make sense of the myriad destinations where missing money collects and how to go about searching for and claiming what is rightfully yours. *The Little Book of MISSING MONEY* makes clear where to look and how to begin your research.

There are millions of dollars being held as unclaimed tax refunds, court settlements, investment accounts, retirement accounts and more. Having worked in the retirement plan industry for more than 30 years, helping people get their money from their retirement plans has always been of particular interest to me. When retirement plans terminate or former employees move and leave their accounts behind, I know how hard it can be to reunite individuals with their money.

I'm also very aware of the growing problem of unclaimed retirement benefits that take the form of uncashed checks. These are benefit distributions that have been made by a plan administrator in an attempt to cash out a former retirement plan participant. For details on this largely unknown source of unclaimed property, read about uncashed/stale-dated checks from retirement plans in the section on Retirement Benefits.

There may be important things money can't buy. For everything else, we work and save all the money we can. When we move, we don't always alert everyone with whom we've ever had a financial transaction of our new address. And when loved ones pass away, it can be daunting to connect the dots back to accounts and other balances held on their behalf. This book provides a great resource to help anyone in this situation get started.

I am grateful for the excellent work Mary Pitman has done to research, share information, and raise awareness of an important issue that has been swept under the rug for too long. Her work has the potential to help tens of thousands of people across the country enhance their retirement nest eggs by reclaiming money that belongs to them. We are proud to support the distribution of this book and hope all who read it will benefit by it – and pass it on!

Peter E. Preovolos, APA, RIA, AIFA, PPC
Chairman & CEO
PenChecks, Inc.
Alpha & Omega, Inc.

# Preface

Linda had a string of bad events happen to her. First, her mother died. Ten months later her husband died. Then someone broke into her son's house and shot, but did not kill, his dog. Linda worked hard as an orthopedic nurse and also had a second job. I knew her because we worked together as RNs.

If anyone could use a break it was Linda.

I was working in the recovery room (where patients wake up from surgery) on a Saturday. I had plenty of time between patients. I spent that time looking up friends, family and strangers on the missing money site. I was actually looking up a doctor who had stopped by that day. He had the same last name as Linda. I entered the last name and city, and was surprised when Linda's name popped up. She had money from an insurance policy, but no amount was listed.

Linda was off that day, but I promised myself that I'd surprise her with the information the next time we worked together. I went up to her floor a few days later.

"I have this hobby," I said. "I like to find money for people on the missing money site. And I found a listing for you." I handed her the paper.

She looked at it, and then looked away. It was a combination of almost crying and being nearly speechless.

"Mary, I've been getting calls and letters from attorneys and firms saying that I had money, but they all want a lot of money to help me get it," she explained. "I was determined to find this on my own, but I didn't know where to begin." She went on to say that one person wanted $700. Another wanted $2,100.

I was appalled that people would be forced to pay what I considered a ransom to get their own money. I assured her I would do everything I could to help her.

As I walked away, I realized she was not alone. There were many more people like her. That was the moment I decided to put all the search tips that I had discovered over the past several years, into a book.

Linda, in the meantime, did a basic search to see if she had other listings. She did. That inspired her to share the information about missing money with the other nurses on her floor. Many of them found money too.

Several weeks later, Linda called me from the post office. "Mary, I have checks in front of me for $63.50, $100, $55.84, and $2,339.80. I've been out of work. I fell and broke my arm in three places. I don't have insurance. I didn't know how I was going to pay my rent," she said, sobbing with relief.

Linda's four checks, totaling $2,559.14, came from a refund, a credit balance, a savings account and a group policy benefit.

In the search process, Linda discovered that her mother had American Express stock from her years as an employee there. The stock, valued at $7,200 at the time, has since grown in value to $7,800. The finder's fee rose to $2,700.

By working with the transfer agent, she learned that she will have to pay probate costs of $285 before the funds will be released.

My initial research for this book centered on individual states. I found multiple ways that names are recorded. The thing is, if you don't enter the name exactly as it's recorded, you'll never find the listing.

I found additional places beyond the state unclaimed property sites. Every time I found one, I thought "I should include this in my book but it doesn't fit with what I'm doing." When I tapped into unclaimed child support payments, I knew I had to rethink my concept for the book.

As I continued my research, I came across many questions people were asking and problems they were encountering in their search for unclaimed money. I decided to find the answers to those questions. This book is the result of that quest.

All the sites I refer to are free to search and free to claim, just like the state sites. I do mention some fee-based services that will help you with specific issues. I am not affiliated with any of them; nor do I get referral fees. In fact, they don't know that I am including them in this book.

I hope you find lots of money, not only for yourself, but also for friends and family. When you start sharing this information, you'll understand the joy I get from helping people. There's nothing like it.

Happy treasure hunting!

*Mary Pitman*

# Introduction

Could you use some extra cash? Are you afraid of getting ripped off? Is this whole missing money thing a scam?

Relax! I'm on your side.

I've made it easy to find legitimate sites that don't charge you. You'll soon see that there are many places besides the state unclaimed property sites where you might find forgotten funds for yourself, family or friends.

You'll find the answers to common questions such as:

- How do I find out if my loved one had a life insurance policy?
- Is there anything I can do to prevent my assets from going to the state?
- Do I have to pay a finder to get my money?
- Will my state take my gift card balance?
- Where do I begin?

I consider myself a consumer advocate on this topic. I wrote the book because my friend was being solicited by finders that wanted fees from $700-$2,100 to help her get her missing money. I felt that was like having to pay a ransom to get your own money.

Keep this book handy because new unclaimed property listings are added all the time. Check at least once a year.

What are you waiting for? Start looking!

---

### ***Fun Fact***

*Unclaimed property is one of the original consumer protection programs.*

---

# The Terminology

There are four terms you need to be familiar with as you go through this book.

**Escheat** refers to items that have met the state inactivity period, generally about 3-5 years. The holder then turns the accounts over to the state which acts as a custodian, holding the monies until you claim them.

**Pre-escheat** is that period of time between the start of inactivity (dormancy) to when accounts gets turned over to the state.

**Holder** refers to the company that has the money that needs to be turned over to the state.

**Owner** is the person to whom the money ultimately belongs.

# Finder's Fees – To Pay or Not to Pay

If you are contacted by someone who wants a finder's fee to put you in touch with your money, the first thing you should do is go to your state unclaimed property site and look for *free*. If you moved, the money may not be in your current state. Some finders provide the last known address. That is the state where you want to search. Go to www.unclaimed. org and click on your state. If you prefer to call or write, the contact information for each state is available on unclaimed. org, on missingmoney.com and in the back of this book. There is no charge if the notification came from the state.

Most states limit what finders can charge. Finders may also be limited as to how soon they can approach you after a listing is posted. It can be as long as two years from when the state receives it. This is so you have a chance to find and claim it for free. These limitations only apply to listings on the state unclaimed property site. They do not apply to property in the pre-escheat phase—the period before it gets turned over to the state.

I have included information about each state's finder's fee laws in the State Contact Information chapter. If you have questions about a letter you received, or a contract you signed, contact the state unclaimed property office or an attorney.

Some finders rely on you not knowing the state law. Be informed!

I have a friend who contacted me after receiving a letter from an attorney who wanted 1/3 of my friend's $10,000+ listing for his business. My friend got him down to $3,000 and felt I was missing out on a huge opportunity by not doing the same.

"You can make a lot of cash doing this," he said.

I explained that this goes against my core belief that people should not have to pay a ransom to get their own money. I directed him to the Illinois unclaimed property site. It took less than two minutes for him to find his listing.

Here's the thing: Illinois only permits a 10 percent finder's fee; plus, the listing has to have been with the state for at least 24 months. Keep in mind the solicitation came from *an attorney*! He was based in Illinois so you would think he would respect the law in his own state.

Even if you don't intend to use one right now, record the contact information for each finder. You don't have to respond immediately to the finder's pitch. Tell him you'll check everything out and get back to him.

Then Google the finder's name. Firms can have more than one Web site, marketing their services to both businesses and individuals. Don't be afraid to dig deep into their Web sites. You may find testimonials from holder companies (those companies that are holding the money) that can provide a valuable search clue, or information that will help you narrow your search.

There is no time limit on when you can claim money that the state is holding for you—except Indiana keeps the money after 25 years. However, it is a common scare tactic to be told that you will lose your money if you don't respond right away. The money may be reaching the end of the pre-escheat phase. Pre-escheat is that time period between the last contact with the owner and the date when the money is to be turned over to the state. Once it gets turned over, it's much easier to find. It's to the finder's benefit to get you to grab the money in this pre-escheat phase. Money held by the city or county usually does not get turned over to the state and often has time limits for claiming. The limitations placed on finders do not apply. Licensing requirements may also be waived.

Although they will not tell you what the listing is or where it is, ask the person who contacted you how long the account has been inactive. Then ask when it is schedule to get turned over to the state. This is necessary information so that you to make an informed decision. There's a big difference between waiting for something that will get turned over in two months vs. two years. If you are told the property will not be turned over to the state, that's a clue as to where to look.

Not everything gets turned over to the state. Some examples are:

- Federal listings such as IRS and HUD refunds

- City, county and state refunds

- Overages from tax sales or foreclosures

- Impact fees

Federal listings must be claimed through the agency that is holding the money. Check with your city or county treasurer if you think you may be due a local tax refund.

If your home was foreclosed or you lost the property due to an inability to pay your taxes, any amount above what is owed is supposed to go to you. Most people are unaware of this. They don't think of giving the Clerk of Court their forwarding address. The check gets sent to the last known address which is the foreclosed home. These listings can be substantial and are a favorite of finders. Check with the Clerk of Court, the county treasurer or tax office.

Finding impact fees that should be refunded can be quite complex. Depending on the wording, the impact fees may get returned to the developer or to the current owner of the property. If the house has been foreclosed, it gets more complicated. There is often no list of these assets.

Finders may claim they can get the money for you faster than if you filed the claim on your own. Not true! As long as you follow the instructions for submitting the claim, yours will be put through at the same pace as the finder's. If you don't include everything the state asks for, then yes, your claim will be delayed.

Many states, such as Texas, require that the finder (or any other term they are using), be licensed and/or registered with the state and have a current sales tax permit.

Check with the unclaimed property division to verify that the finder is allowed to do business in your state. The rules may not apply if they are contacting you about pre-escheat listings or ones that never get turned over to the state.

Massachusetts not only requires their finders to register with the state, but also has a Conflict of Interest clause that states: "No heir finder shall be allowed to register with the Abandoned Property Division and represent the interests of owners if this person or entity performs pre-escheat due diligence work for a holder." [960CMR4.06 (2)]

This means that there are companies that market their services to places like banks and brokerages. They help them identify dormant accounts and deceased owners. This is a good thing for property holders; it helps them comply with abandoned property laws.

The company that provides this service then searches for the owner of the property, using the information it gleaned for the holder. For a 35 percent or more finder's fee, they will connect the owner with the money due. Some search firms market their services to holder companies by advertising on their Web site that the search "is free to you with a reasonable cost to your investors." It is the holder's duty to perform due diligence—making an attempt to locate the owner. To meet that duty, the holder hires the locator firm. But the holder doesn't pay them. You do.

Hopefully the holding companies will start doing the right thing for their customers/clients and list, on their Web sites, the names of those in pre-escheatment, thus giving people a chance to get the full amount of their money before it gets turned over to the state. Many performing rights organizations for actors and musicians do this. If you can hold out, eventually the money will get turned over to the state in most cases.

If the information is about a deceased family member, go through old tax returns. Look for things like a 1099-DIV form that reports dividend income from stocks (you'll need to find the transfer agent, usually available through the company's Investor Relations section); or a 1099-INT form that reports interest which, in turn, would give you a clue about insurance policies, bank accounts or other investments.

Should you decide to use the business that contacted you, know this: You will still have to provide the pertinent documents. If you are a legal heir, you will, in nearly every situation, have to provide a copy of your driver's license, the certified death certificate, and other documents such as a marriage license and/or birth certificate that prove your relationship. If there was a will or trust, you'll need to provide those documents also.

At that point, you've done most of the work. Are you sure you want to give up 35 percent or more? You can always hire someone later to help if you get stuck in the process.

Be aware that there are dozens of websites trying to get people to become a professional finder, touting how easy it is to make money. That's why it's important that you check out the firms that contact you. Some are legitimate, others aren't. This book has become the textbook for many of them.

Consumer protection agencies warn that legitimate search firms do not require payment up front. Inner alarms should go off if someone asks you to pay first; or if the fee is not based on a percentage of the amount collected. All costs should be included in the fee. There should be no additional charges for attorney fees, court costs or anything else.

If you don't feel you are being treated fairly, try to resolve the problem by going up the chain of command at the company. If that fails, you can always file a complaint with the Better Business Bureau in the city where the search firm is located, your state attorney general or with the Federal Trade Commission. Above all, never *ever* pay for an online search.

## *Fun Fact*

*Some states sell their unclaimed property information to finders for a fee.*

# Avoid Missing Money Scams

Here are the top six red flags to alert you to a missing money scam:

1. **It comes as an email.** State unclaimed property offices will not use email to contact you. They simply don't have that information. It's too hard to verify that the email address is truly yours.

2. **It says it's from the National Association of Unclaimed Property Administrators.** NAUPA is a professional organization that the unclaimed property administrators belong to; much like a doctor belongs to the American Medical Association. NAUPA is not involved in reuniting people with missing money, just like you won't get your lab results from the AMA.

3. **You get referred to someone else**. The treasurer handles all claims through its own office. The work is never outsourced.

4. **You're asked for your bank account information**. Granted, in many cases you will have to supply your Social Security number on a form you submit, but NEVER your bank account info. There is no direct deposit with unclaimed property.

5. **There is a fee to file the claim.** This is false for all 50 states and US territories. Legitimate search firms do not charge an upfront fee.

6. **It says it's from me.** I simply do not reach out to people in this manner. You will never, ever get an email or letter from me about this.

## WHAT TO DO
## IF YOU GET ONE OF THESE EMAILS

If you have questions about a contact you received, do not call the number listed. Look up your state unclaimed property office by going to the chapter in this book on State Contact Information, or go to unclaimed.org and click on your state; or go to miss-ingmoney.com and click on the map of the U.S. Scroll down for the state contact info.

If it is found to be false, report it to the Internet Crime Complaint Center at www.ic3.gov and the Federal Trade Commission at www.ftccomplaintadvisor.com.

## LEGITIMATE NOTICES

Imagine my surprise when I received a notice from PricewaterhouseCoopers LLC Abandoned Unclaimed Property Compliance Group stating Google retained them to assist with Google's unclaimed property compliance.

I had money from Google that was about to be turned over to the state unless I replied before the designated date. How could this happen to me?

I changed business checking accounts. I forgot to notify Google. When the direct deposit was attempted, it bounced back to them. They held on to my $51.50 for eight years despite having my email contact and correct address.

How did I know this was not a scam?

There were three things that gave it legitimacy:

1. I had to contact the holder of the money (Google) to get it before the designated date or it would be turned over to the state.

2. I had to log into my Google Merchant Account.

3. No money was requested from PricewaterhouseCooper.

All they asked was for me to verify my address.

---

### ***Fun Fact***

*Unclaimed property laws have been around in the U.S. since the 1930s.*

---

# What's New?

Just when I think I've covered every possible aspect of unclaimed property, I am proven wrong. When I think it's time to send the fourth edition to the printer, there's more to add.

Let's take a look at the new events and some aspects that I missed.

**Cryptocurrency** The State of California filed a class action suit against Coinbank, a cryptocurrency exchange, for allegedly not reporting to the unclaimed property office unredeemed cryptocurrency payments.

I'm the first to admit that I don't understand the concept of cryptocurrency.

The reported transgression occurred when the crypto funds were emailed to people and never redeemed. It's like a business sending you a refund or rebate check that is never cashed. The company doesn't get to keep the money. After the dormancy period is met, the money gets turned over to the state unclaimed property program of the recipient's address. Escheat priority rules state that if the owner's address is unknown, as is probably the case with email transactions, then the money escheats to the state where the company is incorporated. In this case it's California.

In addition, cryptocurrency falls under the category of intangible property which, by law, is escheatable.

The same rules apply to digital currency accounts as a paper money bank account. You *must* have customer-initiated activity to prevent it from escheating to the state. Log in to the account, make a deposit or withdrawal, call to make sure they have your correct address, something, anything that YOU initiate. That shows this is not forgotten. While interest earned on an account is an activity, it does not meet the criteria of "customer initiated." Returned mail used to the criteria to turn something over to the state. But with so many digital accounts the criteria for bank accounts, stocks, bonds, etc. is YOU have to show that you know you have this account. The criteria for dormancy varies by state and in some cases, by the type of property. Your best bet is to have customer-initiated activity once a year. The time it will take you to log in to that account will be far less than the time and hassle of filing a claim. Don't rely on anyone else to do this for you.

**Savings Bonds** Twenty-two states are trying to get savings bonds with addresses in their state turned over to them. The states feel they are in a better position to search for their people. The U.S. Treasury is holding more than $25 billion in bonds, waiting for the owners to come forward. The problem is some of these are decades old. Those entitled to them (if the owner died) may not know they exist.

Not all states actively search for the owners of unclaimed property. In my opinion, if the state does no more than the Treasury Department, then there's no reason to let them have the monies. This is at the Federal Court level.

**Electric Deposits** You may never get your electric deposit back if you don't claim it in a timely manner. Some states, like Texas and New Jersey (possibly more but I just became aware of this) can redirect your unclaimed electric co-op deposit to help pay for utilities for people who are struggling (NJ) or can send a portion to one or more of three funds to help their community: Rural scholarships, economic development, or energy efficiency assistance (TX).

It's one thing if the customers are fully aware of this. It's another if it's in small light print on the back of the utility bill.

I suggest that if you've been on time with your utility payments for more than a year, call and ask to have your deposit refunded in the form of a credit on your bill. This prevents a check getting lost. If they say they can't do that, ask what the process is for receiving the refund when you move. Don't forget to give them your new address so the check can be sent directly to you. I provided a comprehensive checklist at the end of this book to assist you when there's a change of name or address or if you're an executor of a will.

**The Revised Uniform Unclaimed Property Act** (RUUPA) of 2016 was a joint effort of stakeholders in unclaimed property—the states, the holders and insurers—to try to bring some uniformity to these complex issues. It is up to the individual states to adopt the RUUPA in whole, in part or with modifications or reject it entirely.

**Additional sources of unclaimed property** that I never thought about include: Education funds, the court registry, escrow and earnest money, loan collateral, retained asset accounts, suspense accounts where companies place unclassified debits or credits

(it can be temporary or permanent and may involve a wrong account number or an account that has been frozen or deleted.)

Are you ready to start your treasure hunt? If you encounter confusion or get discouraged, remember this: *you are on a no-risk, win-win journey!* Be patient, follow the guidelines I've outlined, and enjoy the hunt!

# 75 SEARCH TIPS

## The Basics

1. The best place to begin is at www.unclaimed.org. Another source is www.missingmoney.com but not all states participate.

2. I get more hits by going directly to the individual states. That's one of the reasons why I recommend unclaimed.org. There can be a lag time between when info appears on the state site and when they upload it to missingmoney.com. In addition, very old listings are dropped from missing money but remain on the state site.

3. To show the difference between the two sites, click on the map of the United States on the missingmoney. com home page. It will take you to a color-coded map. Blue states have their information on the site. Gray states do not. As of press time, the states that do not participate on missingmoney.com are California, Connecticut, Delaware, Georgia, Guam,

Hawaii, Kansas, Oregon, Pennsylvania, Virgin Islands, Washington and Wyoming. In Canada, only the province of Alberta participates.

The advantage of this site is you can search multiple states (if they participate) at once by choosing "Select" where it asks for the state name. The states that don't participate are a lighter gray color on the list of state names. Go directly to any state by clicking on it even if they don't participate. It will take you to the appropriate place. The agency that administers the program varies by state. In Georgia, it's the Department of Revenue. In California, it's the State Comptroller. In Minnesota, it's the Department of Commerce. Clicking on the state will take you to the right place. If you prefer to write or call, the addresses and phone numbers are listed below the map and at the end of this book.

4.  Claims must be filed in the state in which they are held.

5.  You may have money in a state that you never lived in. According to escheat priority rules, the first priority goes to the state of the owner's last known address. If the owner's address is unknown, or if you had a foreign address, the money goes to the state of the holder's corporate headquarters.

6.  What documentation you will need to submit depends

on the type of claim you're making, and what the state requires. At a minimum, expect to send a copy of your driver's license. To get your money as quickly as possible, follow the requirements to the letter! If you omit anything, your claim will be delayed. Before you submit your claim, consider calling the unclaimed property department to verify that you are enclosing everything they require.

7. Save your claim number so you can monitor the entire process. It will make your life much easier if you keep this number in a safe and easily accessible place. If you don't hear anything, it's up to *you* to follow up. The length of time it takes to get the money depends on whether or not there has been a lot of publicity about the unclaimed property program. If you haven't heard back in a month, it's time to check your claim status.

8. Check for missing money *at least* once a year. Just because you did or did not find money previously doesn't mean it won't be there the next time you look. New listings are added all the time. National Find Your Missing Money Day is April 16, the day after you have to pay your taxes. However, you can check at any time.

# The Name Game

9. The less you enter, the broader your search. You can enter as little as one letter in the Last Name box. That will get you a state and an address, or at least a city.

10. The more detail you add, such as middle initial or city, the narrower the search.

11. If your name has an unusual spelling, look under all versions. For example, Elisabeth could also be Elizabeth. My last name is Pitman with one "t." I always look under Pittman also because most people misspell my last name. If the address is correct and it was a company you did business with, then file the claim and explain that the error is on the holder end.

12. If there are multiple common spellings of your name check all of them. For example: Deborah, Debra; John, Jon; Jean, Jeanne, Katherine, Kathryn, Catherine.

13. Look under the formal and informal versions of your name: Catherine, Cathy, Cathie; Robert, Rob, Robbie, Bob, Bobby; Richard, Dick, Rick; etc.

14. If your last name has an apostrophe or other punctuation, search with and without. (i.e. O'Leary, Oleary.) Some states accept the punctuation, others do not.

15. Varying punctuation and spaces can bring up additional listings.

16. If your last name is followed by Jr., Sr., Esq., II, III, IV etc., you would think that those designations would follow the name, right? Not necessarily. While some last name listings may be in that sequence, you can also enter just the ending in the Last Name box.

17. If you have a professional designation associated with your name such as MD, DO, DDS, DMD, DPM, DVM, RN, ARNP, CRNA or anything else, you can enter just that designation under Last Name and you will find listings.

18. Put Mr. or Mrs. (with a period and without) where it asks for the Last Name. The only sense I can make of this is that by putting Mr./Mrs. in the Last Name space, it then puts it at the beginning of the listing so it reads Mrs., John Doe instead of Doe, Mrs. John. The same is true for Spanish salutations: Sr. and Sra. Also check Mr and Mrs, Mr & Mrs, Miss, Ms, Dr. and Rev.

19. Reverse your name. Sometimes listings will be found with your last name first and your first name last.

20. Enter your first name only under the Last Name. It will bring up a state and address or city.

21. Enter your entire name (like on an envelope) under Last Name.

22. Enter Unknown, No Name, Unclaimed, Moved or Illegible under Last Name. See if your address matches any of the listings.

23. Enter Payee under Last Name. This can apply to a business also.

24. Look up all names you have ever used in every state you lived in.

25. You may also have listings that are buried under a bank or brokerage listing. For example:

Banks R Us
FBO Jane Doe
123 Main St.
Any town, USA

Since the first name on the address is the bank, that's what the listing is under. With your name as the next line, it gets put in the address slot and thus is unsearchable by name. This can also be the case with brokerages. (FBO = For the Benefit Of; FAO = For the Account Of)

26. Think about banks you used previously. They may have been taken over by another company and the name has changed. However, the names never change for the listings on the unclaimed property site. For example, if you were a customer of First Union, look under that name and see if there are any listings like the example above.

27. If you were in a car crash and you never got the check from the insurance company, look under the name of the company that the car was financed through. This works the same way as with banks in the example above. Your name may be on the first line of the address.

28. If you were involved in a lawsuit and never received payment, check under the attorney's name. In addition, if the person didn't have any money to pay the judgment against them, look under that person's name. While you cannot claim it, you may be able to get a court order for it.

29. If you were a victim of a Ponzi scheme, look under the perpetrator's name. It may not be there initially but stick with it. The longer they are in jail, the more listings will appear. Notify the trustee as soon as you find a listing.

30. Enter FBO (For the benefit of) or FAO (For the Account of) under the Last Name.

31. Money for trusts can be in unclaimed property limbo. Under Last Name enter: Trust; Irrevocable Trust; Revocable Trust; Rev Trust; Revoc Trust; Living Revocable; Living Trust; Trust Fund, Retirement Trust, Family Trust or The ___ Family Trust. Trusts can also be listed under the date they were started as well as UDT, UTD, DTD, U/A, UA, FBO, TTEE, or Trustee.

32. Enter Safe Deposit under Last Name

33. For children's savings accounts, the person who opened the account is usually listed as a co-owner. Other ways to search include enter UGMA (Uniform Gift to Minors Act) or UTMA (Uniform Transfer to Minors Act) or Custodian, Cust, c/f under Last Name.

34. Don't forget to look up friends and family, including the dearly departed.

35. Speaking of the dearly departed, would you ever think to search using these terms? By now you know there is no limit how a person's money may be listed. If you're searching for money you may be entitled to from a deceased relative, enter these terms in the Last Name:

Estate

(The) Estate of

(The) Est of

To the Estate of

For the Estate of

State of (The 'E' of estate gets dropped)

Deceased

POD (Payable on death)

Trustee

Executor

Beneficiary

No Beneficiary

Unk Heir

Unknown Heir

36. Retirement listings can be found under Roth IRA (all under Last Name) and Last Name: Roth, First Name IRA. Yes, I know there are people named Ira Roth and they will show up. I found a listing for a woman's Roth IRA by searching this way. In this case it was like the example in #25 where the next line was FBO with her name. Also look under IRA, 401K, 403B, Pension or Profit Sharing. Check the chapter on Retirement Benefits for additional places to search.

37. If the listing is very old and you have to send proof that you lived at the address listed but don't have it, you can try:
County tax collector
Utility company
A church where you were a registered member
Voter Registration Office
A school your child attended
College transcript
Driver License Office
Library, if you had a card
Employer
Insurance agent
Professional license
Mortgage company/Bank
Doctor's office records
Old telephone book (at the library)
Credit report— free annually
www.annualcreditreport.com

38. If you're a performer, enter FSO (For the Services of) under the last name.

39. For performers that have a production company, search under the production company name.

40. Payments may be made to the attorney, management company, agent or other professional handling

a performer with the name of the performer following or on the next line. Look under the name of the attorney firm, the attorney's name (full name like on an envelope i.e. Howard Fine), and the agency name.

## *Fun Fact*

*States returned more than $3.2 billion to the rightful owners in FY 2015*

# Charities and Churches

Nonprofits can always use more money to help those in need. Unclaimed property is an easy source of money for most of them. Some of these listings can be decades old. If they were from donors, then these people never got a thank you. Lack of one thank you might make contributors feel unappreciated, resulting in them sending their donations elsewhere. See additional search tips under Businesses and Corporations that apply here.

41. Search as many variations of a charity name as possible. As an example, for The American Cancer Society under the Last Name or Business Name enter: (Follow these examples to search for unclaimed property for your favorite charity)
The American Cancer Society
American Cancer Society
American Cancer
Am Cancer Soc
Cancer Society
Relay for Life

Avon 3 Day
Avon 3 Day Race
Avon Breast Cancer Day
Avon Breast Cancer 3 Day
Breast Cancer 3 day
Breast Cancer Race for the Cure
Breast Cancer Society

There are probably more. This gives a good illustration of how many variations of a name there can be. Remember from #15 above that punctuation and spaces make a difference.

42. Look under the full name of the organization, but also search under the abbreviation it is known by. (e.g. American Heart Association, AHA.)

43. With churches, if part of the name is "Saint" also check "St"—with and without the period. If "First" is part of the name, look up 1$^{st}$ and 1. Shorten the name: Presbyterian, Presby; Methodist, Meth; etc. Don't forget to look for charities associated with your church.

---

## *Fun Fact*

*The largest single payout to an individual in the United States was $32.8 million from a stock claim to a person in Connecticut.*

# Hospitals

With cuts in reimbursements, every dollar counts. Most hospitals have unclaimed property.

44. Look under the hospital's current name and any former name. Many hospitals have changed from XYZ Hospital to XYZ Medical Center.

45. If the hospital is affiliated with a university, look under all variations of the university name. Like the example in #25, when the mail is addressed to the university and the hospital is the second name on the address, the listing goes under the university name.

46. If the hospital is corporate owned, look under the corporation name. Use the tips from the following section on Corporations and Businesses to maximize search results.

47. With so many hospitals buying physician practices, don't forget to look under the physician's name for insurance payments.

48. Payments to doctors may also be listed under the practice name, i.e. Sandy Beaches Urology.

## *Fun Fact*

*Indiana is the only state in the nation that has a time limit for filing claims. After 25 years, they keep your money.*

# Businesses and Corporations

In 2012, Tenneco, a global auto parts manufacturing company in Lake Forest, IL, filed 45 unclaimed property claims for Pullman Co., which it bought in 1996. Shortly after, they received a check from that filing for $8.1 million. It was the largest single payout since the Illinois unclaimed property program began.

From mom and pop businesses to major corporations, this is where the big bucks are. The bigger the business, the more likely it is they have hundreds, if not thousands of listings. You'll never hear this story on TV because people don't care if businesses have money. But business owners and shareholders care.

49. On the state site where it asks for the Last Name or the Business Name, enter the name of a business. Let's use an example of a business that no longer exists: Bear Stearns based out of NY so that's where we'll start. The steps and tips (#50-#57) in this example can be used in any other business search, just as they are presented here.

50. Do the obvious and enter the business name as it is known. If there are more than two words in the name, reverse the order. Under Business Name, enter: Stearns Bear. But wait! There's more!

51. Now enter it as an individual. Last Name: Stearns; First Name: Bear

52. Reverse that. Last Name: Bear; First Name: Stearns

53. Now put both names under the individual Last Name: Bear Stearns. Leave the First Name blank.

54. You guessed it! Reverse it by switching the names still leaving it under the individual Last Name: Stearns Bear. First Name is still blank.

55. Allow for typos such as Bear Stern.

56. When there are two or more words in the name, eliminate the space between them. Bearstearns

57. Drop the last letter from the name. When people are typing the name quickly, the last letter can get dropped. If there are two or more names in the business, drop the last letter from each word individually. Bear Stearn, Bea Stearns.

58. If there are more than the maximum that the state will show, (California shows the first 500 listings, North Carolina 250, Texas 200, etc.), work your way

through the alphabet like this: Name of company (space) A; repeat (space) B; and so on. This will let you find the maximum for each entry.

59. Under Last Name enter Co, Company, Corp, Corporation, Inc, LLC, Ltd.

60. If your company has "and" in the name, enter the name with "and," "&" plus try it without it.

61. Enter these as Last Name, First Name: Payable, Account(s); Receivable, Account(s); enter them in the entirety under Last Name: Account(s) Payable; Account(s) Receivable; Payroll. Sometimes the name of the business will be in the address. In most cases, you simply have to search for your business address. (s) means search with and without the 's.'

62. Search under Payroll.

63. Sometimes the account is listed as Store #123 or Store 123. There's even one where it spelled out the numbers—Store Forty One O Two in Texas. (Ring a bell with anyone?) When the address begins with the store number and then the name of the business follows, the listing goes under the first line of the address (refer to #25). In this case it's the store number.

64. Follow the corporate history and look up every company involved. For example: May Dept. Stores became Federated Dept. Stores that took over Macy's. They are all there. This is an especially important concept when it comes to banks. All the banks that no longer exist such as Barnett Bank, First Union, South Trust, etc., have dormant money being held by the states. You can research bank "genealogy" by going Wikipedia and searching List of Bank Mergers in the United States. Sometimes there are customer names as co-owners attached to bank and brokerage listings: ABC Bank and John Doe

65. Even businesses that have gone under such as Circuit City, Linens 'n Things and Toys r Us have listings. If you are one of the subordinated debt holders that filed a claim against bankrupt/failed companies, then these listings are a good thing for you to bring to the attention of the bankruptcy court.

66. If your loved one or family member is being released from jail, don't forget to get the balance in the commissary account, especially if you contributed to it.

# Local, State and Federal Government

Cities, county and states can always use more cash. Unclaimed local, state and federal money is an important area to research. This is a part of the missing money story that never gets reported.

But first, let's look at where you might find money for yourself in the local coffers.

67. Check with your city or county auditor or treasurer to see if you have a refund due from your taxes. These listings do not get turned over to the state but there is a limited time to claim them.

68. If you lost your home because you couldn't pay your taxes and the tax lien/deed sold for more than you owed, you are entitled to the overage. Check with the tax assessor's office to see if you have money coming. Be sure the property tax office has an address where you can be reached.

69. The same holds true if you had a foreclosure. For example, if you owed $110,000 on your home, but it sold for

$150,000, the excess is yours. Check with your mortgage lender or the clerk of court where the foreclosure was recorded. If the home hasn't sold yet, be sure both have an address where you can be reached.

70. Search for unspent impact fees through the building department or planning and zoning division.

71. If you've been current with your utility payments (water, gas, electric) for at least a year, ask to have the deposit refunded.

Now let's look at where you may find money for your local/state government.

72. David Sarokin, a contributor on *Yahoo Voices*, has one of the best search tips I've come across. Do a Google search like this: "city OR county of" and "unclaimed property OR money OR funds." So many times, a Google search will bring up fee-for-service paid listings. This one actually brings up the names of cities and counties.

73. Look for your local schools, both public and private, plus law enforcement agencies and fire rescue.

74. Look for any state-specific programs in your state. For example, MediCal in California or Peach Care in Georgia.

75. Bringing it closer to home, keep the name search broad. You can usually limit it by city. Keep in mind that most cities started out as "Town of…", "Village of…" or "Municipality of…" so don't forget to try those searches. Look under the following names:

City of/Town of/Village of

Name of city

County of

Name of county

County Commission

County Court

State Court

Name of state

State of

Council of

Board of

Dept. of

There may be others I haven't thought of. Let your imagination run wild!

## **_Not So Fun Fact_**

*Gift card balances*
*are taken by some states.*

# 108 PLACES TO LOOK
## The Government

**Search your Federal government.** There are listings for every department of the federal government that I could think of. There may be some obscure office somewhere, but the big ones are all have listings: Social Security, Medicare, Veterans Administration, Homeland Security, all branches of the military and even the Internal Revenue Service.

**Social Security Administration** When earnings are posted under an incorrect name or social security number, the Office of Central Operations does not post the earnings to an individual's earnings record. Instead it holds the money in an Earnings Suspense File until it knows the worker's correct name or social security number. As of October 2014, the money held is a staggering $1.2 **trillion** dollars in uncredited wages for 333 million W2s from tax years 1937-2012. Most of this is attributed to the use of false Social Security numbers, usually by illegal immigrants.

There are also simple typos. Anytime numbers need to be manually entered, like when you fill out the W-4 with your new employer and they enter it into the computer, there is a risk of the number accidentally being entered incorrectly. While knowing this may not get you immediate cash, when your payments into the program are not credited to you, it can affect the benefits you receive when you retire or if you become disabled. When you get your W-2 or 1099 at the end of the year, verify the social security number is correct. If it isn't, notify your employer who will need to notify social security and the IRS of the error and report the correct earnings as well as issue you corrected statements.

**Savings Bonds** There are almost 70 million unredeemed savings bonds held in the Treasury Department for the American public worth $25,409,842,680 as of June 30, 2019. Many of them have stopped earning interest. That's like stuffing your money in a mattress.

To search, you'll need the social security number of the owner of the bonds. The owner and the buyer of the bonds is not necessarily the same person. The Treasury

Department does not actively search for bond owners. States have been trying to take possession of the savings bonds to make it easier for their citizens to find and claim them. In 2013 Kansas was the first state to file in state court to gain access to bonds that were purchased with a last known address in Kansas. The appeal is now in the Federal Circuit Court of Claims. They are awaiting a ruling as we go to press. In total, 22 states have passed legislation. Ten are at the federal court level with three more states waiting to join the federal case.

*(From public domain text on the U.S. Treasury Website.)*

- Each year, 25,000 payments are returned to the Department of the Treasury as undeliverable.

- Billions of dollars in savings bonds have stopped earning interest but haven't been cashed. If you have savings bonds, Series A, B, C, D, E, F, G, H, J, K, Series EE (issued Jan. 1, 1980-Jan. 1, 1989), Series HH (issued Jan. 1, 1980-Jan. 1, 1999) or Savings Notes, they have all stopped earning interest. Cash out or reinvest them so your money can start working for you again.

- Matured, Unredeemed Debt and Unclaimed Moneys: https://www.treasurydirect.gov/foia/foia_mud.htm

- This site provides information on what to do for undeliverable bonds for those that were lost, stolen or destroyed. https://www.treasurydirect.gov/forms/sav1048.pdf

- Email queries to the Treasury Department about lost savings bonds. When you contact them through their web site, the transmission is encrypted so it's secure, according to the information provided. Queries must be less than 5,000 characters. https://www.treasurydirect.gov/email.htm

- To find out if a savings bond has been cashed, write to:
  Treasury Retail Security Site
  P.O. Box 2186
  Minneapolis, MN 55480-2186.

- **Treasury Retail Securities Services Locator** If you have a question about Treasury Bills, Notes, Bonds or TIPS call (844) 284-2676 (toll free), recorded information is available 24 hours a day and customer service representatives answer questions from 7 a.m. to 6 p.m. Eastern Time, Monday through Friday, except holidays. If calling from outside the United States, call (304) 480-6464. You can write to them at:

Treasury Retail Securities Services
P.O. Box 9150
Minneapolis, MN 55480-9150

- Due to the Privacy Act of 1974, if you are not the owner or co-owner, the Treasury Department is limited in the information it can provide. If you are a legal heir, contact them and see what you need to submit.

**Bearer Bonds and Registered Securities** balances total $125,346,154.15 Bearer bonds are unregistered, meaning there is no record of the owner's name. If you're holding a bearer bond, it's yours.

The last definitive security was issued in 1986 and matured in May 2016. Approximately one percent or less of the total matured securities are redeemed each month. It's time to check your financial portfolio!

**Workers Owed Wages** I'll share a personal story about this.

I was about 19- or 20-years old working as the manager of the largest department at King's Department Store in West Palm Beach Florida. I found out that the guy who was the head of hardware was making $1 per hour more than me and hadn't been there as long as I had.

I filed a complaint with the Equal Employment Opportunity Commission for sexual discrimination and also filed a complaint with the fantastic folks at the Wage and Hour Division (WHD) of the U.S. Department of Labor.

Let me tell you, those folks do not mess around. They came in and pulled records from seven years back: Who was hired and at what rate? Who got raises? How much were they and how often did they get them? Who was fired? Why? The company was fined. Many employees were entitled to back pay. I got $1,500 which was a lot of money in the mid-70s.

This is one of those hidden gems that you have to know about. When a situation like this happens, some of the people involved may have left during that seven-year period they researched. If they were entitled to compensation the WHD holds the money while they try to find the person. If they can't find them after 3 years, they are required to turn the money over to the US Treasury.

Check your former employer here  https://webapps. dol.gov/wow/

**Veteran's Administration** VA benefits are only benefits if you take advantage of them. Some of these benefits do not involve getting money. They are simply free services that I feel are important to share. Here are some of the highlights:

- Vietnam Veterans diagnosed with a disease recognized as being related to exposure to Agent Orange may be eligible for service-connected compensation. http://www.publichealth.va.gov/exposures/agentorange/

- VA's National Suicide Prevention Hotline is available 24/7 for those feeling alone, depressed or hopeless. (800) 273-TALK (8255)

- Vets4Warriors is a peer-to-peer suicide prevention counseling service geared toward members and veterans of the National Guard. Help is available 24 hours a day by calling (855) Vet-Talk (838-8255) or online at www.vets4warriors.com. It is staffed by veterans trained as counselors and is available to all branches of the military.

And there's a lot more. Go to http://www1.va.gov/opa/myva/index.asp

Coaching into Care is a telephone program started in 2011. It is a telephone service that provides assistance to family members and friends trying to encourage their Veteran to seek health care for possible readjustment and mental health issues. It's a national phone service that places priority on linking Veterans with benefits and services available in their own communities. If you think your Veteran friend or family member is having a difficult time and could benefit from readjustment counseling or mental health care, please utilize the Coaching into Care service: call (888) 823-7458 or email CoachingIntoCare@va.gov

For information on VA life insurance, go to the chapter on Life Insurance. Find information about survivor aid and benefits here: http://www.vba.va.gov/survivors/agencies.htm

For information about the Radiation Exposure Compensation Act (RECA) go to the Compensation Funds chapter. RECA coverage is limited to the atmospheric nuclear testing program conducted by the United States after World War II, those who worked in uranium mines and downwinders. Survivors of eligible participants may be able to file a claim for the one-time lump sum settlement. **The deadline to file a RECA claim is July 9, 2022.**

**Financial Management Service** (*Based in part on public domain text from the Financial Management Services*

*Web site*) There is no government-wide, centralized information service or database on how unclaimed government assets can be obtained. Each individual federal agency maintains its own records. The titles and addresses for all federal agencies are available in The United States Government Manual, available in the reference section of most public libraries. You must determine the type of benefit or payment that could be involved, the date on which the payment was expected, and how the payment should have been made. Given this information, the agency responsible for certifying any payment due should be able to assist you in determining the current status of any payment involved.

Professional finders file a Freedom of Information Act request to obtain the information on checks that are returned to the government. There is a check number provided, but no information about to whom the check was issued, or the amount. They then file another FOIA requesting the issuing information on the returned check number. This has the name of the person and the amount of the check. With that information, they search for the owner of the property. http://www.fms.treas.gov/faq/unclaimed.html

**IRS Refunds** Never got that tax refund? Go to www.irs. gov. Click on "Where's My Refund?" on the right. You'll need your Social Security or Taxpayer ID number, the filing status and the exact whole dollar amount of your return. You can also call (800) 829-1040, but you'll still need the information listed above. If you select direct deposit for the refund, there is no chance of it getting lost in the mail, plus you will get the refund quicker.

The good news is that if you completely forget about a refund, it will catch up with you the next year when you file.

Once you file your taxes, there is no time limit to claiming a refund. If you are due a refund, you have to file your taxes within three years. If you miss the deadline, the government keeps your refund. Don't let that happen!

# Courts

**Court Registry** The court registry holds funds such as cash bonds, funds in dispute, money for a minor until the child reaches age 18, restitution owed to a victim in a criminal case, surplus money from a trustee's sale, garnishments, child or spousal support, criminal bail, civil bonds, investment earnings, and civil judgment payments. If your home goes to foreclosure and sells for more than what was owed, this is where the money gets deposited.

These funds can become forgotten. What happens to these unclaimed accounts varies by state.

Florida, for example, considers the money unclaimed after five years. If the entitled party does not claim it, the money gets turned over to the State Treasurer who deposits it into the State School Fund. The entitled party can claim the money from that fund, but the interest earned stays in the fund.

In Washington, unclaimed funds for restitution get turned over to the County Treasurer. If the funds are for non-restitution, they get turned over to the Washington State Department of Revenue.

In all cases, a court order is needed to release the funds. Contact the Clerk of the Court or your attorney for assistance. The Clerk of the Court cannot provide legal advice, but they can tell you what your next step is.

Most importantly!! Make sure your address is up to date with the U.S. Post Office and the Clerk of Court.

**Unclaimed Criminal Restitution** The California Department of Corrections and Rehabilitation (CDCR) currently collects $400,000 monthly for victims who have been named in court orders as being entitled to restitution paid by the criminal who committed the crime. Often, the information sent to CDCR by the county courts does not include victim address information to let CDCR know where to send the money collected. However, state law provides that victims can come forward at to claim restitution collected on their behalf. There must be a court order to receive this money. Visit the CDCR website for additional information: http://www.cdcr.ca.gov/Victim_Services/ unclaimed_restitution.html or call: (877) 256-6877; or email: victimservices@cdcr.ca.gov

To find out more about this fund in your state Google Unclaimed Criminal Restitution with the name of your state.

**U.S. Bankruptcy Court** More than $280 million dollars is waiting to be claimed. If you are a creditor of a person or corporation that has declared bankruptcy, you may have unclaimed funds. Upon providing full proof of the right to funds held by the court, a claimant may obtain an order directing disbursement of unclaimed funds 28 U.S.C. 2042.

After five years, the money gets returned to the Treasury Department under the claimant's name. There is no time limit to claim it. Contact the bankruptcy court where the case was filed for instructions. Check http://www.uscourts.gov/court_locator.aspx to find the bankruptcy court where the case was filed.

On top of that, most businesses that have closed their doors due to financial failure have listings on the state unclaimed property sites with the majority being in the state where the business was incorporated. That is something you can bring to the court's attention if you are still owed money. There are also listings for Bankruptcy Court/US Bankruptcy Court on the state unclaimed property sites. Some of those may have been from the debtor and should be credited to their debt.

To see if there are unclaimed funds in your name even if you filed decades ago, go to https://ucf.uscourts.gov

Each state's forms vary slightly so it's best to ask that the proper form be sent to you. It's called Petition to Claim Unclaimed Funds from the US Treasury. You'll need to have it notarized. Notary services are usually available for free at your bank or your insurance agency.

You can stay on top of the court actions regarding your claim as a creditor by signing up for Electronic Bankruptcy Noticing, a free service that allows court notices to be transmitted electronically delivering them faster and more conveniently. Sign up for it here: http://ebn.uscourts.gov/index.adp

**Canadian Bankruptcy Court** You can search by debtor or creditor name through the Office of the Superintendent of Bankruptcy Court. http://www.ic.gc.ca/cgi-bin/sc_mrksv/bnkrptcy/ud/ud_srch.pl

**Class Action Lawsuits** Have you ever received one of those postcards in the mail stating that you may be entitled to a proposed settlement from a class action lawsuit and then you never hear anything else?

It used to be that more than 90 percent of class action lawsuit funds went unclaimed, but that's been changing in the positive direction for consumers for the past 10 years according to Scott Hardy, president of Top Class Actions. Search this site for settlements. It's free for consumers. Submit your claims on open lawsuits at https://TopClassActions.com. When a class action settlement closes, that's it. If you didn't submit your claim, you're out. You can sign up for their free newsletter to stay up on the latest cases.

**Child Support Payments** I brought an unclaimed child support listing that was on the Summit County, Ohio site to the attention of Elisabeth Leamy, the consumer reporter from *Good Morning America* that did the *Show Me the Money!* segments. She followed up on it.

The mother received $8,249.50 that the county had been holding for her for the previous two years. She was also going to continue to receive payments of $332 for the next six years making her total take $31,821.

If you owe child support payments and have listings on the state unclaimed property site, you may never get to see that money. More and more states are enacting legislation to allow the unclaimed property funds to be intercepted when the owner is behind on child support.

In addition to listings with the state, other funds can be confiscated from federal and state tax refunds, lottery winnings, passport denials, or accounts identified through the Financial Institution Data Match. For more information on the FIDM, go to http://www.acf.hhs.gov/programs/cse/fct/fidm/parents/what_is_fidm.html

Another aspect of child support are payments that were made to the child support office but perhaps the case number was wrong or the name of the recipient was illegible. These funds sit stagnant in the child support offices because they don't know who to credit.

Don't forget to keep the child support folks informed of your change of address or name so you get your money. Putting in a change of address with the post office doesn't get the information to the child support office unless their envelope states Address Correction Requested. Even then, it can be missed. A change of address with the post office lasts for one year.

One more thing, you can enter Child Support in the Last Name; there are listings. Perhaps money you are owed has not made it to the child support office and is being held by the state. Encourage them to check.

Here are some direct links:

**Illinois** Cook County: Search by name or case year, division code and case number. www.cookcountyclerkofcourt. org/?section=CASEINFOPage&CASEINFOPage=4310

**Ohio** Franklin County Auditor: There are more than just child support payments here. You can also find lost heir accounts, vendor payments, proceeds from Sheriff's sales, Restitution payments and jury/witness fees. https://www. franklincountyauditor.com/fiscal/unclaimed-funds

**Ohio** Summit County: The list is updated every 6 months. https://co.summitoh.net/prosecutor/index.php/component/ content/article/13-child-support-enforcement-agency-divi-sion/139-oct-2015-unclaimed-funds-report

**Oregon:** Holds on to the funds for two years prior to turning it over to the state.

**South Carolina:** Contact information for undeliverable child support payments that were returned by the post office because of a bad address.
https://dss.sc.gov/child-support/parents-families/parents-links-and-resources/undeliverable-child-support-funds-list/

**Wisconsin:** As of February 5, 2019, there were more than 4,400 names listed. Go here: http://www.statetreasury.wisconsin.gov Click on Search for Missing Money. Under Search and Claim you will find unclaimed child support. You can also call (608) 266-9909 or write to them at Department of Children and Families, Bureau of Child Support, P.O. Box 7935, Madison, WI 53707-7935

For child support offices in all 50 states plus state Native American tribal support contacts, go to

https://www.acf.hhs.gov/css/resource state-and-tribal-child-support-agency-contacts

A handbook for military families is available to help with their unique child support needs. http://www.acf.hhs.gov/programs/css/resource/a-handbook-for-military-families

---

### *Fun Fact*

*So far, no state has returned more unclaimed property than it has taken in.*

---

# Banking, Financial Services, Stocks

**Stocks** If you think losing track of your stocks could never happen to you, consider this—the largest single listing returned to an individual in U.S. history was $32.8 million from more than 1.25 million shares of stock. Before that it was $6.1 million for a woman who didn't know that her family had stocks. Before that $4 million from stocks. It *can* happen to you!

Transfer agents handle the administrative work of stocks. If you are contacted by a search firm and determine that it may be about stock that you own, you can find the name of the transfer agent by visiting the investor relations section of the company's website. Contact the transfer agent directly and see if you can intercept it before it goes to the state. In Canada, try the Canadian Stock Transfer Company here:

https://ca.astfinancial.com/InvestorServices/Unclaimed-Assets?lang=en

The stocks or mutual funds are either in possession of the transfer agent or in the possession of the state.

Transfer agents in the U.S. must comply with SEC Rule 17Ad-17 of the Securities Exchange Act of 1934 which requires them to search for all lost shareholders. It's called "due diligence." Two searches are required.

The first is done between 3 and 12 months of an account being identified as lost. The second search is done 6-12 months after the first search was completed. Some states are using customer inactivity instead of returned mail to decide a shareholder is lost.

The gray zone in this comes when the due diligence is performed. The state laws about what a finder can charge do not apply until the money is in the possession of the state. This means the finder can charge whatever they want. Although some states, like North Carolina, have laws that state that pre-escheat contracts are unenforceable, the finder firms get around that by saying they are based in another state and operating under that state's laws.

Shareholders are a favorite market of professional finders. The finders, charging fees of 30-35 percent, are poised to make a great deal of money. There's one company that markets to the transfer agents promising "there's no cost to you and only a modest cost to your shareholders." So, although it is the transfer agent that is required by law to perform the due diligence, they don't pay for it. You do.

It's all in the name of "keeping the money from going to the state." If you wait for it to go to the state, you get your stocks for free. However, waiting for it to go to the state means it can still fluctuate with the market. That may work for you or it may work against you.

Check the escheat rules for your state. Do they use the returned mail criteria or customer inactivity? Many states are trending toward decreased dormancy periods from five years down to three years. Some states cash in stocks as soon as they hit the unclaimed property office regardless of what the market is doing. After all, it's in the state's interest to have the cash in their pocket.

You have several options to prevent this from happening:

- Vote your proxy.

- Log in to your account once a year. Just going to the web site doesn't count. You must log in with your password.

- If there is a 24-hour automated line, call and use your PIN to check your balance.

- Call and speak to a customer service representative.

- Respond immediately to all letters regarding account inactivity.

- Make a transaction on your account at least once a year. Automated programs such as dividend reinvestments plans do not legally prove control over the account.

- Cash all dividend and redemption checks.

- Update your address when you move. Returned mail will trigger inactivity status in some states.

- Make a list of your assets and where they are so if you die unexpectedly, your family has some idea of what to look for.

**Investors Claims Funds** (*Based on public domain text on the SEC Web site*) are managed through the Securities and Exchange Commission. This page lists the SEC enforcement cases in which a Receiver, Disbursement Agent, or Claims Administrator has been appointed. Funds that are recovered and available for investors will be distributed according to an approved plan.

In addition to seeing whether a claims fund has been established, you may want to find out whether a private class action has been filed against the company you invested in. If you're aware of violations of the securities laws, please report it to the SEC by using the online complaint form.

If your broker-dealer has gone out of business, you can visit the website of the Securities Investor Protection Corporation (www.sipc.org) to find out whether your firm is the subject of a liquidation proceeding and how you can obtain a claim form. www.sec.gov/divisions/enforce/claims.htm

**National Credit Union Administration** (*From public domain text on the ncua.gov Web site.*) When a credit union with federal insurance is liquidated, NCUA's Asset Management and Assistance Center (AMAC) is responsible for paying the share accounts to the members. Share accounts claimed within the 18-month insurance period are paid at their full insured amount. At the expiration of the 18-month insurance period, shares that are not claimed are considered uninsured and written down to share in the loss to the NCUSIF. Even if shares are uninsured when they are claimed, there may still be a distribution.

On rare occasions, the liquidation of a credit union may result in surplus funds. If a surplus remains, a distribution to the shareholders is required. This may occur several years after the credit union is liquidated and it is sometimes difficult to locate these members. If you had an account at a credit union that closed, go to www. ncua.gov and search Unclaimed Deposits.

**Federal Deposit Insurance Corporation (FDIC)** When a participating bank fails, the FDIC acts as receiver until the new bank takes over, as Chase did in 2008 when Washington Mutual failed. The dormant accounts, in this case defined as those that have not had activity for three years or more, were sent to the state of the customer's last known address.

Under the Federal Unclaimed Deposits Amendment Act, the FDIC turns unclaimed accounts from failed banks over to the state of the account owner's last known address for a 10-year custodial period. If the account holder's address is unknown, it gets turned over to the state where the financial institution is incorporated under the account holder's name. After the custodial period the money is returned to the FDIC and you lose any right to claim it.

When a failed bank or savings and loan federal deposit insurance is liquidated, the FDIC resolution division is responsible for paying:

• Unclaimed insured deposits up to the insurance limit

- Dividends declared on the excess deposits over the insurance limit

- Dividends declared on general creditor claims

- Funds distributed to the shareholders of the institution

- Search by your name, business name, the bank name, city or state. For details, go to https://closedbanks.fdic.gov/FUNDS/FundsNET/Funds

In many cases these funds remain unclaimed because:

- The insured deposit is never claimed from the assuming financial institution.

- The dividend check on the excess deposit amount is not cashed.

- The dividend check on the general creditor claim is not cashed.

- A valid address is not on file and the dividend check has been returned to the FDIC.

## **Housing and Urban Development/FHA refunds**

*(Based on public domain text on the HUD Web site)*
HUD is not liable for a distributive share that remains

unclaimed six years from the date the notification was first sent to the last known address of the mortgagor.

Also, really important is that the rules governing eligibility for premium refunds and distributive share payments are based on the financial status of the FHA insurance fund and are subject to change.

You may be eligible for a refund of a portion of the insurance premium if you:

- Acquired your loan after Sept. 1, 1983

- Paid an up-front mortgage insurance premium at closing, and

- Did not default on your mortgage payment
  (Review your settlement papers or check with your mortgage company to determine if you paid an up-front premium.)

You may be eligible for a share of any excessive earnings from the Mutual Mortgage Insurance Fund if you:

- Originated your loan before Sept. 1, 1983

- Paid on your loan for more than seven years, and

- Had your FHA mortgage insurance terminated before Nov. 5, 1990

(There are some exceptions. To see if your name is associated with a refund go to <u>https://entp.hud.gov/dsrs/refunds/</u> )

**<u>Safe Deposit Boxes</u>** When the fees on a safe deposit box go unpaid for 3-5 years, the contents of the box get turned over to the state. The state in turn lists it on the unclaimed property site for a period time that varies by state. Eventually, items of value are sold at auction and the money is held for the owner when the claim is eventually made. Back rent for the box is usually deducted from the proceeds of the auction.

The unfortunate aspect is, in most states, items of sentimental value such as love letters, photographs or a lock of baby's hair get trashed. Some states honor the value of military medals and have laws that prohibit them from being sold at auction. Instead, they work with veterans' organizations to reunite the owner or family with the military medals.

Here is some useful safe deposit box information I received from a banking professional.

"Request a box high up, especially in coastal regions or in areas prone to flooding. Putting your paperwork in zip lock bags can be helpful. Fire is another monster as most vaults are fire resistant, not fireproof. Most people believe the FDIC covers the contents of their box and this is not true. If it can be proven that a loss was due to a bank employee, then the bank's insurance kicks in."

And then I was told something that was completely counter intuitive. This may save you a lot of headaches when your loved one dies. "You should never place the only copy of your will in a safe deposit box unless you know what your state laws are about entering a box after the death of a lessee as sometimes, they can block entrance, even if your name is on the box." Check with your bank to find out what the state laws are. You still want to have another person authorized.

Don't forget to include information about your safe deposit box on your list of assets, including the bank branch and where the keys are kept.

---

## Fun Fact

*States hold auctions of tangible property such as the contents of safe deposit boxes. Some are live auctions; some are on eBay.*
*The money is held for the owners.*

---

# Performance Royalties

If you are in the entertainment business and receive royalties or residuals for your work, be sure you have a beneficiary assigned to receive that money in case something happens to you—like death. A named beneficiary supersedes anything in your will!! Keep this information updated.

In other news …

The Music Modernization Act (MMA) became law on October 11, 2018. The purpose is to streamline how music licensing and royalties are paid with regards to online streaming music and media services.

For the royalties where the person who earned them cannot be found, the money will be held for three years. After that, the rightful person can lose all rights to any royalty. It will be called unclaimed accrued royalties.

Royalties have been "streaming" in and accruing in the US until this issue was resolved with the passage of the MMA. The estimated cache is nearly a billion dollars!

For these old royalties that have been held, the time frame to potentially lose the rights to then is as little as one year.

Make sure your contact information is current! Don't rely on others to do this for you. Update your information annually.

## Preventing lost royalty payments

Two words: Direct deposit. Given the mobile nature of the artist's life, it's the best way to make sure your money reaches you. Of course, this depends on your paperwork being in order.

Eric Beall, author of *Making Music Make Money: An Insider's Guide to Becoming Your Own Music Publisher,* offers these tips to make sure your music is registered properly and that you get all the royalties that are yours:

- Check your registrations. Then check them again. BMI, ASCAP, and Harry Fox all have systems that allow you to check that your song is registered correctly. Even if you're signed to a publishing company, you still need to check and re-check those registrations. A publisher has a responsibility, but in many cases not a legal requirement, to register your songs. This is not an area for blind faith. Trust, but verify.

- Make some friends. Get to know your ASCAP, BMI, or SESAC representatives. If you do a lot of business in the UK, then make some contacts at MCPS/PRS. You need to know people, and just as importantly they need to know you. Low profile is no profile.

- Act fast. I'm amazed at how many writers have a hit, then spend a year or two trying to decide if they want a publishing deal, who they should sign to, what society they want to affiliate with, etc. All the while, the money being earned by the song is languishing in "copyright control" or "unclaimed earnings." If you put a $1000 on the sidewalk, would you expect it to be there a year later? Time is of the essence.

- Major recording companies may also have royalty listings. Check with the company that the artist was signed with. If the information is not available online, call and inquire.

Did you catch search tips #38-#40 in the beginning of the book?

**There's an App for that!** BandPage is a Facebook app created by RootMusic that partnered with SoundExchange to put royalties in the hands of the artists that have earned them. SoundExchange connects with the bands on BandPage to let them know about the money they may be due. Artists must register with SoundExchange to get the money flowing their way.

## MUSIC PUBLISHING

**EMI Music Publishing** If you have questions, call the royalty hotline (212) 830-2079 or email usa.royaltydept@emimusicpub.com

**Sony Music** Update your address or make inquiries about your royalty payments here: https://www.sonyatv.com/en/missing-royalties

**Universal Music Publishing Group** The Royalty Help Line is (888) 474-4979 or you can email them at umpg.royalty@umusic.com. The link for Royalty Central where you can find FAQs, address updates and search for your unclaimed royalties is https://www.umusicpub.com/us/Digital-Music-Library/Royalty-Central.aspx

**Warner Music Group** If you are a royalty participant and believe you are entitled to an accounting or have moved without notifying WMG, fill out the royalty information request form by going here: http://www.wmg.com/artistroyalties

## PROFESSIONAL ORGANIZATIONS/UNIONS

### The Alliance of Artists and Recording Companies

AARC collects and distributes featured artist royalties to more than 500,000 members worldwide under the Audio Home Recording Act of 1992. It requires that users or digital audio copying devices pay royalties, a portion of which is distributed to artists. The royalty comes from the sales of blank CDs and personal audio devices, media centers, satellite radio devices and car audio systems that have recording capabilities. https://www.aarcroyalties.com/

**SAG/AFTRA Royalties** As a performer or heir/beneficiary of a performer you may be due US or foreign royalties/residuals. Call (855) 724-2387 or go to https://www.sagaftra.org/residuals-portal

**APRA** Australasian Performing Rights Association and the Australasian Mechanical Copyright Owners Society also has information about royalties. Enter "Royalties" in the search box at http://apraamcos.com.au/

**Director's Guild of America** has money from foreign levies, a list of deceased members to whom at least $50 is owed and non-members to whom at least $25 is owed. There's also an option for non-members to register non-covered works for informational purposes only; but it may help determine to whom payments are due. http://www.dga.org/ForeignLevies.aspx Call (310) 289-5328 or email questions to foreignlevies@dga.org.

**Writer's Guild of America** allows you to search the foreign levies program by writer's name for whom the Guild is holding foreign levies but lacks payment information; by title for which the Guild is holding foreign levies but has not identified the writer or lawful heirs; or you may provide the Guild with information about a non-WGA project that you believe may entitle you to foreign levies. https://www.wga.org/the-guild/levies-payments/foreign-levies-program

To check your residuals, go to http://origin.www.wga.org/. Click on Member Support on the right, then Look Up Residuals. You can also search for undeliverable funds the Guild may be holding for you at: https://apps.wga.org/undeliverables/

**Recording Artists Royalties** is a joint project of the American Federation of Musicians (AFM) and American Federation of Television and Radio Artists (AFTRA). A list of individuals that have been credited for covered sound recordings is available at: https://www.afmsagaftrafund.org/ Click on Unclaimed Royalties on the top bar.

**PERFORMING RIGHTS ORGANIZATIONS**
**American Society of Composers, Authors and Musicians (ASCAP**) ASCAP members can log into their account via 'Member Access' to see if a royalty distribution check was issued, as well as to make sure that their information is current. www.ascap.com

**Broadcast Music, Inc. (BMI)** Update your address or sign up for direct deposit here: http://www.bmi.com/address
In addition, if you are the legal heir of a deceased BMI affiliate, the information you need to file for the

royalties is at www.bmi.com Enter "Estate" in the search box.

BMI songwriters can register their set list, no matter the size of the venue, for possible royalty payments at https://www.bmi.com/special/bmi_live

**SESAC** is another Performing Rights Organization like BMI and ASCAP, but it is by invitation only. http://www.sesac.com

**SoundExchange** is an independent digital performance rights organization that collects statutory royalties from satellite radio (such as SIRIUS XM), internet radio, cable TV music channels and similar platforms for streaming sound recordings. The Copyright Royalty Board, which is appointed by The U.S. Library of Congress, has entrusted SoundExchange as the sole entity in the United States to collect and distribute these digital performance royalties on behalf of featured recording artists, master rights owners (like record labels), and independent artists who record and own their masters. If you are an artist or a sound recording copyright owner, you may have royalty payments waiting for you, especially if you haven't registered with them. Check here: http://www.soundexchange.com/artist-copy-right-owner/does-soundexchange-have-royalties-for-you/ SoundExchange has paid out more than $5 billion in royalties. Please note that they are authorized by regulation to release older unclaimed listings to offset their costs. If you're a musician and you're not registered with them you may lose money you never knew you had.

---

# *Fun Facts*

*New York is holding $16 billion in unclaimed property.*

---

# Retirement Benefits

*Contributed by Peter Preovolos*

With retirement benefits, as with life insurance policies, make sure your beneficiary contact information is current and your family knows about this asset. If you changed jobs and left your retirement plan with your former employer, pay close attention to this chapter!

First, a little background . . .

## Uncashed/Stale-Dated Checks from Retirement Plans

The actual assets – whether cash, stocks, bonds or mutual funds in employer-sponsored retirement plans such as 401(k), 403(b), profit sharing, stock bonus plans and a host of others – are held in trust by a corporate institution that acts as a custodian of the funds. The custodian can be an individual, such as the president of your former employer's company, or a corporation, such as a bank, brokerage, insurance company or mutual funds firm.

When an employee participating in the retirement plan leaves his/her job, retires or dies, the employer instructs the custodian to pay the participant their money. The money is transferred from the plan to the custodian's general ledger, and a check is issued to the participant's last-known address provided by the employer. Taxes can be withheld depending on whether the check was made to a rollover account or paid out as a lump sum benefit. Since most plans (with the exception of a Roth IRA) are based on pre-tax dollars, the taxes are paid when the money is withdrawn if it is not being rolled over.

When checks go uncashed or get returned because of a bad address, employers are rarely notified by the custodian unless they ask the custodian whether the account has any uncashed checks. Otherwise, the money stays with the custodian, earning interest for the custodian but not the plan participant. Thus, the custodian has no incentive to track down the rightful owner of the funds.

The money and taxes that were withheld are not returned to the plan but do get reported to the IRS. The custodian has three years to restore the funds and taxes, after which the window of opportunity is closed forever. In the absence of redepositing the funds into the plan, a default IRA may be set up.

In most cases, an uncashed check where taxes are withheld is grossly unfair to the participant because the taxes get paid without their knowledge. Unless the participant files a tax return within three years (highly unlikely), the IRS keeps the money. The participant doesn't get credit for the taxes paid, and never sees their money again.

Furthermore, the Employee Retirement Income Security Act (ERISA) of 1974 mandates that plans with 100 or more employees must be audited. However, the auditors are not required to audit the outflow of cash, which means the money doesn't get reported to the plan sponsor. As a result, the plan sponsor is unable to instruct the custodian to return the funds, and if taxed, submit a claim to the IRS to restore the taxes so that portion of the account balance can be returned to the plan or a Default/Auto Rollover IRA can be established.

At this point, one might ask why the funds aren't escheated to the state of last-known residence. The Department of Labor (DOL) frowns on this and has repeatedly stated that these funds – even if they have been taxed – are considered qualified money and there-fore exempt from being escheated. This is in contrast to dormant savings accounts, CDs and certified checks issued by a bank, which must be escheated after the bank has made several attempts to contact the account holder to verify whether the account is active or dormant. However, the bank has no obligation to report money sitting in a trust account, and state regulators do not have the authority to look for money in those accounts.

**What Can Plan Participants Do?** Take control! Don't lose your funds by leaving this money behind.

When you leave a job, roll over your retirement plan to your new employer, or set up a personal IRA. Your local bank or other institution can help you with this, as a rollover is not the same as a withdrawal. The receiving institution usually does not charge a fee to set up a personal IRA. However, there may be a fee for processing the transfer of the money out of the plan.

If you decide to leave your funds in the former employer's plan, at least update your contact and beneficiary information with the plan administrator and your employer. However, if your account balance is less than $5,000, your former employer has the right to remove you from the plan by establishing a Default/ Auto Rollover IRA.

Check your income tax returns for discrepancies between what the IRS says you received and paid. This could be the only red flag you see, and a tipoff that somebody paid taxes on your behalf.

Employers can play an active role by requesting an annual accounting of all uncashed checks from the custodian of their plan assets. For plan administrators (the custodian), not returning the money can be considered a violation of their fiduciary responsibility. The same may be said of the employer that gave the order to make the payout and did not follow up at least annually to determine that all checks processed from the plan were cashed and the participants received their money.

If you can't find your money even after searching the sites listed in this book, contact the plan administrator – the bank, brokerage, insurance company or mutual funds firm – that was handling the account. If you don't remember the name of the institution, contact your former employer

Keep in mind that plans and human resources personnel change, and current personnel may not know who was handling the 401(k) plan 10, 15 or 20 years ago. If you can't identify the institution, search the state where you worked by checking their escheatment registry. There is also a joint registry of all states available at www.unclaimed.org. Then go to the National Registry of Unclaimed Retirement Benefits (www.unclaimedre-tirementbenefits.com) in the possibility that your former employer registered you and your benefit with NRURB.

Financial institutions change as well. A list of bank mergers is available on Wikipedia. https://en.wikipedia.org/wiki/List_of_bank_mergers_in_the_United_States

Given the changes that have occurred in business and financial institutions, you may not be able to find what shouldn't have been lost in the first place. But don't let that stop you from looking!

**Terminated 401(k) Plans** If the company you worked for terminated the 401(k) plan and could not find you, your money may have been sent to a company like PenChecks Trust. Remember that in terminated plans the $5,000 ceiling disappears, allowing the employer to transfer any amount solely because the plan has been terminated.

A Qualified Termination Administrator (QTA) is responsible for terminating the plan.

The DOL grants approved institutions – who must be a bank, insurance company, brokerage firm or mutual funds company – the ability to act as the QTA, and provides specific guidelines they must follow when terminating the plan. These include using search methods that look at state records to see if the company still exists, searching for the former officers of the company, and more.

Once the plan has been adjudicated as abandoned (terminated), the financial institution must begin communicating with all current and former employees to notify them of their benefit entitlement and how to obtain their money. When former employees can't be located, the QTA will roll over the money into a Default/Auto Rollover IRA that can only be invested in an insured FDIC deposit account. By regulation, the money may not be put at risk.

In the absence of being able to find a custodian that will accept a Default/Auto Rollover IRA, the employer may establish a taxable savings account. However, today many financial institutions offer Default/Rollover services, so chances are small that the employer would transfer your forgotten money into a taxable savings account. IRA funds can only be escheated to the state when the participant reaches age 70½, at which time the law mandates the beginning of required minimum distributions from the account. Those funds become eligible to be escheated, and the DOL no longer considers them qualified funds.

You can also search for information about terminated plans by going to the Department of Labor Employee Benefits Security Administration: https://www.askebsa.dol.gov/AbandonedPlanSearch/

## **National Registry of Unclaimed Retirement Benefits**

The U.S. Department of Labor states that $850 million in 401(k) plans go unclaimed every year. The NRURB's goal is to help working people reunite with their rightfully earned money. All searches for unclaimed assets on the NRURB website are anonymous and secure.

The National Registry is a nationwide, secure database listing of retirement plan account balances that have been left unclaimed. However, unlike terminated plans, these are active plans with inactive participants. Former employees can perform a free, secure search to determine if they are entitled to any unpaid retirement account money. Employers can register (for free) the names of former employees who have left money with them. Search by social security number at www.unclaimedretirementbenefits.com.

Accounts registered with NRURB are strictly voluntary by former employers and institutions; there is no mandate for them to register. However, if the funds are turned over to PenChecks Trust Company of America, that participant's IRA will automatically be registered with NRURB.

**<u>Pension Benefit Guaranty Corporation</u>** The PBGC acts as the custodian of defined benefit pension monies that come from bankrupt or terminated corporations that sponsored a defined benefit plan. Today, PBGC holds more than $400 million dollars in unclaimed pension benefit funds for over 80,000 participants. In 2015 PBGC paid out more than $5.6 billion to 840,000 retirees. Their website even has listings for bankrupt companies like Enron and Eastern Airlines.

Defined benefit pension plans promise to pay a specific monthly amount to participants when they retire. If you participated in one of these plans (not a 401(k), 403(b) or profit-sharing plan) in a privately-owned company that terminated and then transferred the plan to PBGC, you may have money.

Even if you don't know whether the pension was transferred to PBGC, it doesn't hurt to look! If you are a legal heir to someone who had a pension, you may be entitled to claim the money.

Search by the last name of the participant, the name of the company, or the state in which the company was located. Like all of the sites identified in this book, this one is free to look up and free to claim. It is not a list of people due pensions from PBGC. It only lists those people whom PBGC has not yet been able to contact directly. https://www.pbgc.gov/search-unclaimed-pensions

In addition to defined benefit plans, Congress has recently authorized PBGC to accept unclaimed benefits coming out of a terminated or abandoned defined contribution retirement plan, such as a 401(k), ESOP (Employee Stock Ownership Plan) or profit-sharing plan and transfer them into a Default/Auto Rollover IRA.

*Thank you, Peter Preovolos, APA, RIA, AIFA, PPC, Chairman & CEO PenChecks, Inc for sharing your extensive knowledge on this topic!*

**Thrift Savings Plans** are the federal government's equivalent of 401K plans. If you or a deceased family member participated in this program, check for any balance by going to http://www.tsp.gov or call (877) 968-3778.

## Federal Employees Retirement System/ Civil Service Retirement System

If you leave your government job before becoming eligible for retirement you can ask that your retirement contributions be returned to you in a lump sum payment; or if you have at least five years of creditable service, you can wait until you are at retirement age to apply for monthly retirement benefits. This is called deferred retirement. http://www.opm.gov/retirement-services/

**U.S. Railroad Retirement Board** Survivors of retired railroad employees that died between 1964 and 2001 may be entitled to receive a $2,000 life insurance benefit. Claimants can call MetLife at (800) 310-7770 to determine eligibility. MetLife is solely responsible for determining if a claimant meets eligibility requirements. For online benefit information go to www.rrb.gov/mep/ben_services.asp

**NY State Deferred Compensation Plan** If you have two or more checks outstanding, issuance of further checks may be suspended. Call (800) 422-8463 to check.

**SC Retirement System Unclaimed Funds** If you ever worked for an employer covered by the Retirement Systems in South Carolina or left the covered employ-ment more than one year ago and left your money in your retirement account, then search this site for inactive accounts or call (803) 737-6800   https://online.retirement.sc.gov/MemberAccess/welcome

**WI Retirement Benefits** Participants in the Wisconsin Retirement Fund have 10 years to file for their benefits or the money reverts back to the state. Here's the press release about it as well as a link in the story to search by name. http://wistatetreasury.wordpress.com/2012/05/08/searching-for-owners-of-abandoned-wisconsin-retirement-funds/

**Other State Retirement Programs** Each state has its own site for state retirement benefits. Google the name of your state and retirement benefits.

## *Fun Fact*
*The U.S. Treasury is holding Savings Bonds that date back to the 1930s.*

# Life Insurance

## (US and Canada)

It is estimated that more than $1 billion dollars goes unclaimed every year due to lost or unknown life insurance policies. The average claim is about $2,000 with some as high as $300,000. In 2015 life insurance companies paid out $74.5 billion.

I found money from my father's estate as stock in an insurance company. I had a question and contacted them. I learned there was also a life insurance policy that listed my half-sister as the beneficiary. It was only by that chance call that the policy came to light and she was able to file and get her money.

If you don't know if a loved one had one or more life insurance policies, here are six steps you can take.

1. Start with the agency they have their car or homeowner's insurance policy through. Look for insurance cards from insurance agents or any paperwork or policies. If you find a policy but can't find the

insurance company that is listed, *Best's Insurance Reports* is available in the reference section in most libraries. It contains information about mergers and name changes in the insurance industry.

2. Check their canceled checks for any premium payments to an insurance company. Don't forget to check the bank statement for any payments that were made electronically either to or from the insurance company.

3. When you're closing out the deceased's banking matters, ask their bank if they had a safe deposit box. If you don't have a key, you'll be charged to have them drill out the lock.

4. Check with former employers for any group life insurance policy your loved one may have participated in. If he or she was a union member, check with the union. Also check groups such as AARP or professional organizations they belonged to.

5. Review past IRS returns looking for a 1099-INT form for interest reported from an insurance company.

6. An often overlooked source is credit cards or the auto insurance policy that may carry an accidental death benefit. If your loved one died from an injury or accident, look into this.

The last recourse is look company by company. The state insurance office has a list of companies that operate in that state. Remember to search in each state where your loved one lived and may have purchased a policy.

There was a multi-state lawsuit against major life insurers for not turning over unclaimed life insurance benefits to the state. What came to light was that the insurers were using the Social Security Death Master File to determine when an annuitant died and they could stop making payments. However, they were not using the very same database to determine when a policy holder died and they needed to make a payout to a beneficiary. In addition, when payments on the policy stopped, they would debit the account for the unpaid premium. In some cases, this resulted in completely depleting the account.

As a result of the lawsuit, the insurers reinstated those policies to the value at the time of death. Insurers now check the DMF quarterly. However, the death still needs to be verified. If the benefit isn't claimed in three years, then it gets turned over to the state.

Right now, update your beneficiary contact information. You may find the person listed has already died or it may be an ex-spouse or some other person that you don't want the money to go to. Keep in mind, minors can't receive this money. It needs to go to a trust in the child's name with a custodian and a trustee designated.

Some of the older whole life policies begin losing value after the policy holder reaches age 95. Read the fine print in the policy or check with your insurance agent. Go back to the search tips in the beginning of the book and look at #35 for a list of additional ways to search for unclaimed property in the deceased's name.

**No insurance company should charge you a fee for searching their records.**

**The American Council of Life Insurers (ACLI)** has tips for how to determine if your loved one might have had a life insurance policy. Go to: www.acli.com/ACLI/ consumers/Life+Insurance/Locating+a+Missing+Policy/ default.htm

**New York Life** Unclaimed funds can include uncashed checks from dividends, premium refunds and over-payments, insurance benefits/policies, health benefit payments, trust funds, and estate proceeds.
https://www.newyorklife.com/my-account/unclaimed-funds-finder/

These are only the policies that have met the escheat criteria and were turned over to the state. If the policy is in the pre-escheat phase, it would still be held by the company. Contact them directly if you think your loved one had a policy through them.

**John Hancock** It says you will get a response within 7-10 days of your query.
https://www.johnhancock.com/forms/account-search-request.html

**MetLife** The policy owner and the insured may not be the same person.
https://www.metlife.com/policyfinder/

**Veterans Life Insurance** The VA holds returned life insurance payments, such as those for death benefits, dividend checks, or premium refunds indefinitely. There are approximately 3,000 unclaimed policies totaling $30 million. The unclaimed funds are from the following policies:

- United States Government Life Insurance (USGLI 1919-1951)

- National Service Life Insurance (NSLI 1940-1951)

- Veterans Special Life Insurance (VSLI 1951-1956)

- Veterans Reopened Insurance (VRI 1965-1966)

- Service-Disabled Veterans Insurance (S-DVI 1951-Present)

- Check Veterans Affairs at:  https://www.insurance.va.gov/UnclaimedFund

The Unclaimed Funds Search does not include funds from Servicemembers Group Life Insurance (SGLI) or Veterans Group Life Insurance (VGLI) policies from 1965 to the present. It is administered by the Office of Servicemembers Group Life Insurance (OSGLI) with Prudential.

- SGLI/VGLI contact information:

    **Phone:** (800) 419-1473, M-F 8-5, Eastern Time
    **Email:**  osgli.osgli@prudential.com
    **Website:** https://giosgli.prudential.com

- Survivor aid and benefits for military families can be found through the VA here: http://www.vba.va.gov/survivors/agencies.htm

**Survivor Benefits** is another category of benefits for heirs after a loved one's passing. For example, when a Federal employee or retiree dies, monthly or lump sum payments may be payable to survivors. Categories include: Deceased Employees, Death of a Spouse, Deceased Annuitants, Deceased Survivors, Child Beneficiaries, and Students.

You can learn about these death and survivor benefits by going to: http://www.opm.gov/retirement-services/csrs-information/survivors/#url=Death-Survivor-Benefits

**Federal Employee Retirement System Death Benefit**
A basic employee death benefit may be available to a spouse, former spouse or child.

**Surviving Spouse** If an employee dies with at least 18 months of creditable civilian service under FERS, a survivor annuity may be payable if:

- the surviving spouse was married to the deceased for at least nine months, or
- the employee's death was accidental, or

- there was a child born of the marriage to the employee.

The spouse may be eligible for the Basic Employee Death Benefit, which is equal to 50% of the employee's final salary (average salary, if higher), plus $15,000 (increased by Civil Service Retirement System cost-of-living adjustments beginning 12/1/87). The $15,000 has increased to $32,423.56 for deaths on/after December 1, 2016.

**Former Spouse** The Basic Employee Death Benefit may be payable to a former spouse (in whole or in part), if a qualifying court order, awarding a benefit, is on file at OPM and the former spouse was married to the deceased for a total of at least nine months and did not remarry before reaching age 55.

Monthly survivor benefits may also be available for children. Check here: http://www.opm.gov/retirement-services/fers-information/survivors

U.S. Office of Personnel Management
Retirement Operations Center
P.O. Box 45
Boyers, PA 16017
(888) 767-6738 (7:40 a.m. -5 p.m. ET)
retire@opm.gov

This contact info is also good for questions regarding the Civil Service Retirement System.

Some states have websites to help families search. Life insurance policies are issued in the state the person was living in when the policy was written.

**The State of New York** has created a web site to help people find policies that were issued in NY. https://www.dfs.ny.gov/consumer/lost_policy_find.htm

**Ohio Department of Insurance** makes it easy for family to find out if their loved one bought life insurance while living in Ohio.

You can print the forms you need online by going to http://www.insurance.ohio.gov/Forms/Pages/Consumer-Forms.aspx

You want either form INS2502 Missing Life Insurance/Annuity Search Request, or form INS0501 Missing Life Policy Coordinator Contact Information. Print the request form. Fill out the form and have it notarized. Send it in with a copy of the certified death certificate.

If you don't have Internet access call (800) 686-1526 to request that a claim form be mailed to you. To request the form by mail, write to:

Missing Life Insurance/Annuity
Search Request Service
Ohio Department of Insurance
Consumer Affairs-Life Unit
50 West Town St., Suite 300
Columbus, OH 43215

The department forwards your request along with the supporting documentation to all Ohio-licensed life insurance companies within 25 business days of receiving your request. You must be a beneficiary or executor of the estate to request this information.

**The Louisiana Department of Insurance** site has useful tips for determining if someone had a life insurance policy and the company that issued it. You can only search for policies that were issued in Louisiana and then contact the insurance company for further information. The site cannot be used to search for policies that were not purchased in Louisiana. You will need the deceased's social security number and date of death when you call. Go to:

http://www.ldi.la.gov/consumers/insurance-type/life-annuities/life-insurance-policy-search

## National Association of Insurance Commissioners

This is a free search. Companies participate on a voluntary basis. It may take up to 90 business days for a reply. https://eapps.naic.org/life-policy-locator/#/welcome

**Be sure to check the topic of Escheat Estates in the Miscellaneous Money chapter.**

The companies listed below will perform a search for a fee: **MIB** searches life insurance companies that are members of their organization. If your loved one had a policy with a company that is not a member of MIB, the search will not show the policy. The fee is $75. When they return their findings to you, you will also get the *Policy Locator Research Primer* that will provide additional sources for you to check. Go here: https://www.mib.com/lost_life_insurance.html

**The Lost Life Insurance Finder Expert** charges $108.50 but searches more than 420 companies. The extent of their involvement is to help you with the submission, submit the query and answer any questions you may have. The companies reply directly to you. Go here: www.l-lifeinsurance.com

**FindYourPolicy.com** Michael Hartmann, a licensed life insurance agent, created this site after his father's passing. People can register the name of the company that they have a life insurance policy with so loved ones can find the information in a central location and know who to contact. It's free to register your information but searches are $19.95. Part of the fee goes to cancer research. www. FindYourPolicy.com

## Canada

### Canada Life/Great-West Life

Listings can include claim payments, policy payouts or premium refunds.

https://www.canadalife.com/about-us/consumer-information/unclaimed-property.html

**Sun Life Canada** All the information you need to submit an unclaimed property query regarding insurance or investment products with Sun Financial or its predecessor companies is available here:

https://www.sloc.co.uk/slfuk/Customer+services/

If you had a policy in Canada through a company that no longer exists, go to the Canadian Life and Health Insurance Association website. http://www.clhia.ca

# International Unclaimed Property

The United States isn't the only country with unclaimed property.

## CANADA
### Bank of Canada

Contact the Bank of Canada for any search concerning an unclaimed balance in an account in a financial institution or a deposit with a federally chartered trust corporation. The Minister of Revenue does not have jurisdiction over such property.

Federally regulated banks or trust companies turn the money over to the Bank of Canada when the account is deemed dormant. Bank of Canada holds balances of $1,000 or more for 100 years. Balances of less than $1,000 are held for 30 years.

As of December, 2018, there were 2 million accounts worth $816 million. The oldest accounts date back to 1900. https://www.bankofcanada.ca/unclaimed-balances/

**British Columbia:** They have listings worth $140 million including one that goes back to 1859. On the Web site, click Search for Unclaimed Property and then "Other Sources." It will take you to an extensive list of additional sites in Canada. www.unclaimedpropertybc.ca

## Quebec

As of January 22, 2019 Quebec, has 360,949 accounts worth $332,999,816.

https://www.revenuquebec.ca/en/unclaimed-property/searches/register-of-unclaimed-property/

**Alberta**: Does not report how much is held or has been returned. Claims must be submitted within 10 years of when the listing was received.

https://www.alberta.ca/unclaimed-property.aspx

**Nova Scotia Intestate Unclaimed Funds:** When people die in Nova Scotia without a will (intestate) or their heirs cannot be found the money is transferred to the Minister of Finance where it is held for 40 years. After that, the government is allowed to take it. Search the database here:

http://www.novascotia.ca/finance/en/h ome/financialservices/unclaimedfunds/default.aspx

**Nova Scotia Credit Union Deposit Insurance Corporation:** Search for unclaimed balances here:

http://www.nscudic.org/unclaimedbalances/index.html

**Bankruptcy Court of Canada:** Unclaimed Funds Database
http://www.ic.gc.ca/cgi-bin/sc_mrksv/bnkrptcy/ud/ud_srch.pl

## THE UNITED KINGDOM
### England
Assets are very conservatively estimated to be £77 billion.
www.unclaimedassets.co.uk/
Also try: www.mylostaccount.org.uk/

**Child Trust Funds:** If a child was born between September 1, 2002 and January 2, 2011, they might have Child Trust Fund money. There are about one million unclaimed Child Trust Funds worth more than £1.5 billion. Detailed information is available at http://www.unclaimedfinances.co.uk/overview-unclaimed-child-trust-funds.html When vouchers were issued but not used, HRMC opened an account in the child's name. HRMC ceased issuing vouchers in October 2012. If you don't remember the provider, you can get help by contacting HM Revenue and Customs. https://www.gov.uk/child-trust-funds Although the Child Trust Fund is no longer operating there still may be money available to claim.

**Bona Vacantia:** (means "ownerless goods") administers the estates of those who died intestate without known kin and collects the assets of dissolved companies and failed trusts. Check the list here: https://www.gov.uk/government/organisations/bona-vacantia

**Pension Tracing Service:** helps folks find lost workplace and personal pensions in the UK. The estimated value is £19.4 billion. 800,000 pensions worth £9.7 billion have gone unclaimed by owners or heirs. Call 0800 731 7888 M-F 8am-6pm. For Welsh, call 0800 731 7936. Visit www.gov.uk/find-pension

**Unclaimed Assets Register:** through Experian UK provides a resource for individuals, solicitors and businesses to find out if they have lost pensions, insurance policies or investments. You have to create an online account for a small fee. The web site is www.uar.co.uk or you can call them at 0333 000 0182

**SCOTLAND**

**Citizens Advice:** will do a benefit check for you to see if you may be entitled to benefits or tax credits that you are not aware of. CA advisers regularly find cases of people missing out on some sort of benefit or grant just because they weren't aware of it. www.cas.org.uk

## IRELAND

Search the National Treasury Management Agency www.ntma.ie Use the Search box. Enter Dormant Accounts Fund.

## EUROPE

### France

Association Française des Banques (Only available in French but the page can be translated.) www.afb.fr/Web/internet/interMain.nsf?OpenDatabase

### Switzerland

Swiss Banking www.swissbanking.org Use the Search box. Enter Dormant Assets. This site will give you details about filing the claim: www.dormantaccounts.ch/narilo

### Greece

Although Greece does not have an unclaimed property program for forgotten accounts, I did find information from an attorney about abandoned real estate in Greece. It may be possible to get it back. I know nothing about this attorney. This is for informational purposes only. https://www.helleniccomserve.com/country.html

## AUSTRALIA

**Australian Securities and Investments Commission:** There is more than $1.1 billion in lost shares, bank accounts and life insurance. www.fido.asic.gov.au/fido/fido.nsf/byheadline/Unclaimed+money+-+overview?openDocument

## Australian Tax Office's SuperSeeker:

site for lost superannuation accounts
http://www.ato.gov.au/superseeker

## New Zealand

Inland Revenue Department www.ird.govt.nz/unclaimed-money

## AFRICA

## Kenya

As of March 31, 2019, the trust account at the Unclaimed Financial Assets Authority https://www.ufaa.go.ke had a value of $39,329,817,347 KShs and 1,454 safe deposit boxes. (One U.S. dollar equaled 102.15 Kenyan shillings on June 25, 2019.)

## Uganda

Was considering implementing an unclaimed property program at the time this book went to press.

## CARIBBEAN
## Jamaica
Dormant accounts are held by the institution for 15 years. After that, the money is turned over to the government. Jamaica has $45 billion in unclaimed assets and is preparing to take $15 billion of that for the government because people have not claimed it in the allotted time frame.
http://www.mof.gov.jm/documents/documents-publications/document-centre/file/1656-unclaimed-bank-balances-2018.html

## Cayman Islands
Cayman National Bank lists dormant account numbers and the date the account was opened. https://www.caymannational.com/dormant_accounts_notice.html

## Eastern Caribbean
If dormant accounts have no activity for 15 years, the money goes to the state. Eastern Caribbean Central Bank publishes a list of their dormant accounts. Member countries include Anguilla, Antigua and Barbuda, Commonwealth of Dominica, Grenada, Montserrat, Saint Kitts and Nevis, Saint Lucia, Saint Vincent and the Grenadines.
www.eccb-centralbank.org/statistics/abandoned-properties

## ASIA

### Israel

Administrator General and Official Receiver. The National Unit for Location and Management of Property manages various types of assets including real estate, personal property and money. https://www.justice.gov.il/En/Units/AGOR/Pages/The-National-Unit-for-Location-and-Management-of-Property.aspx

### Malaysia

Contact the Registrar of Unclaimed Moneys http://www.anm.gov.my/index.html

### India

Dormant accounts, stocks and real estate are not turned over to a government agency but you can get help through www.fundtracers.com for a fee.

### Japan

Japan is in the process of implementing an unclaimed property program. It is expected to be up by the end of 2019.

# Compensation Funds

**9/11 Victim Compensation Fund** provides compensation to any individual (or personal representative of a deceased individual) who suffered physical harm or was killed as a result of the terrorist-related airplane crashes on Sept. 11, 2001, or the debris removal that took place in the immediate aftermath.

On February 15, 2019, the Special Master determined that the funding remaining in the VCF would be insufficient to pay all pending and projected claims under current VCF policies and procedures. On July 29, 2019, President Donald Trump signed a bill guaranteeing funding until 2092. https://www.vcf.gov The Helpline is (855) 885-1555.

**Radiation Exposure Compensation Act (RECA)** is program administered through the Department of Justice. It has paid more than $2 billion in claims. The Act's coverage is limited to the atmospheric nuclear testing program conducted by the US after World War II. The Act only provides lump sum compensation for an individual who has contracted a covered cancer following their exposure. It may apply to three populations:

- Uranium miners, millers and ore transporters ($100,000)

- Onsite participants at atmospheric nuclear weapons tests ($75,000)

- Individuals who lived downwind of the Nevada test site ($50,000)

**The deadline to file a RECA claim is July 9, 2022!**

Uranium mine worker claims are paid from the Energy Employees Occupational Illness Fund. It has no set expiration date and will be replenished as needed.

Further details are available at http://www.justice.gov/civil/common/reca.html

For proof of participation as an on-site participant, send for your film badge radiation history. Form NSO-192 plus the Privacy Act form you'll need are available to download from a site listed below that is run by John DeBusk, an atomic testing veteran.

Nuclear Testing Archive

National Security Technologies, LLC (NSTec)

Contractor to the United States

Department of Energy

Mail Stop 400

P.O. Box 98521

Las Vegas, NV 89193-8521

If the participant is deceased, surviving family members can complete the Surviving Relative Affidavit. Both of these forms are available at www.angelfire.com/ tx/atomicveteran. This site has lots of useful information, more than I can include on this topic. If you prefer to call to request the forms, the number is (800) 729-7327. You'll also need to request the Privacy Act Form. Do not try to file this through the Veterans Administration as that is the wrong agency.

I strongly encourage you to go to the Angel Fire website listed above for help with some of the problems you are likely to encounter.

**Holocaust Survivors** Holocaust survivors or the victims' heirs may have assets from before the Holocaust they don't know about. This has nothing to do with the state unclaimed property sites. This is important because the survivors are elderly and dying. There are 60,000 assets including:

- **Real Estate** – apartments, buildings, land plots, and subdivided land in Israel

- **Monies** – accounts opened in Israeli banks, shares and bonds. Monies acquired through the sale or expropriation of real estate, and the compensation received from profitable assets rental fees on apartments and land.

- **Jewish Colonial Trust (JCT) Shares** – Shares in the Jewish Colonial Fund established by Benjamin Ze'ev Herzl in 1899 to serve as the Zionist Movement's financial arm.

- **Contents of safes and art pieces**

For information about Holocaust victims' unclaimed bank accounts, insurance funds, art and more, call the Holocaust Claims Processing Office in the New York State Banking Department at (212) 709-5583 in the U.S. or (800) 695-3318 outside the U.S. The web site is: https://www.dfs.ny.gov Enter HCPO in the Search box.

The Company for Location and Restitution of Holocaust Victim Assets (www.hashava.info) was started in 2007 under law in order to do historical justice with the victims of the Holocaust and reinstate with their legal heirs those assets located in Israel that were purchased before they found their death under the Nazi regime. They ceased this service under law on December 31, 2017. However, there is a wealth of information still available such as contacts for the information center for the Restitution of Assets; the Holocaust Survivors Rights Authority in the Ministry of Finance; the Ministry for Social Equity (for commemoration); and the Administrator General in the Ministry of Justice who deals with Holocaust Victims Assets. All of these are in Israel. You can also see if your relative's name in on the list of those with assets in Israel.

The Claims Conference on Jewish Material Claims Against Germany is another site. Go to: www.claimscon.org

All deadlines to file claims relating to the Swiss Banks Settlement have expired. All claims and appeals through the International Commission on Holocaust Era Insurance Claims have also expired as of December 2006. The site, www.icheic.org, is maintained as a historical record.

**<u>Vaccine Injury Compensation Program</u>** Individuals who believe they have been injured by a covered vaccine can file a claim against the Secretary of the Department of Health and Human Services in the U.S. Court of Federal Claims seeking compensation from the trust fund. Eligible claimants can recover compensation for vaccine injury-related medical and rehabilitative expenses, pain and suffering, and lost wages. Since the program began in 1988, more than 6,000 claimants have been awarded a combined total of more than $3.9 billion. Details can be found at: http://www.justice.gov/civil/common/vicp.html

**<u>Disaster Money</u>** The Exxon Valdez oil spill of 1989 was a major disaster. There are still more than 1,800 people that haven't claimed their money. Some of them may be deceased by now, but the heirs should look into claiming the funds. Exxon has turned the remaining money over to the state unclaimed property site.

**<u>Victims of Violent Crime</u>** Most states have a Crime Victim Compensation Program to help with medical bills, loss of earnings and even funeral expenses. This applies to children too. Check with your local victim advocate for more information. You can also

Google the name of your state followed by Crime Victim Compensation.

**Compensation from airlines** This isn't a compensation fund but it's about compensation you're probably not aware of for flight interruptions. A company called AirHelp (https://www.airhelp.com/en) will tell you if you're entitled to financial compensation for things like overbooking, delays, cancellations, missed connections, denied boarding or delayed baggage. This may go back to 3 years! They also have a free app, AirHelp. You can scan your boarding pass and it will let you know your status. Here's a secret . . . Sometimes weather delays aren't really weather delays. They also have rankings for airports and airlines. Their fee for dealing with the airlines is 25 percent. They only get paid if they get money for you. This is available for international flights too.

I love this line from their website: "We believe that air passenger rights weren't made for airlines to interpret on a whim."

# Miscellaneous Money

**Gift Cards** You finally decide to use that gift card you've been holding on to. You make your selections and hand the clerk your gift card. You're told, "There's nothing on it." You know it hasn't been out of your possession. No one else used it. So, what happened?

The balance was probably turned over as unclaimed property. But here's the catch: Since gift cards are purchased anonymously, where do you look?

Start with Delaware.

Escheat priority rules state that if the owner's address is unknown, as is the case with gift cards, then the money gets turned over to the state where the business is incorporated. More than 60 percent of public companies are incorporated in Delaware. If it's not there, find out where the company is incorporated and check that state's unclaimed property site. You may have to call and have them look for it.

The Revised Uniform Unclaimed Property Act of 2016 decided to leave the decision about gift card and gift certificate balances up to the individual states. An excellent resource for checking the gift card rules in your state is https://www.classaction.org/gift-card-laws. To keep up to date with the laws as they change, check the National Conference of State Legislators, http://www. ncsl.org/research/financial-services-and-commerce/ gift-cards-and-certificates-statutes-and-legis.aspx

Here are some tips to help you get the most from the card:

- Look for an expiration date. Even if the gift card has expired, ask the merchant if they will still honor it.

- Read the fine print on the card to see if there are any fees.

- If you purchase a gift card, save the receipt in case it is lost or stolen. You *may* be able to get it replaced.

- If you're purchasing a gift card for someone, make sure it is a place where they would want to shop. An elderly person may not want to shop online if there is no store in their area. If it's for a restaurant, make sure there is one near the recipient. Or choose a Visa card that can be used anywhere. Your recipient may need basic things like food or gas, not more stuff.

- Ask which state the gift card was purchased in and

check its unclaimed property law at the site referenced above.

- Some states will allow you to request that small balances (usually less than $5) be given to you in cash, but you have to ask for it.

- If you receive a gift card you won't use, there are sites where you can sell or trade it. Top Ten Review gives a side-by-side comparison of the top 10 exchange sites. https://www.toptenreviews.com/gifts/seasonal/best-gift-card-exchange-sites/

- Use it before you lose it!

## ESCHEAT ESTATES

**Oregon** has a division for escheat estates. An escheat estate is property remitted to the Department of State Lands when a person listed in a will or an heir to the estate cannot be located, or refused to accept the estate at the time of the estate's probate. A court may direct an attorney or personal representative of an estate to pay or deliver the property to the Estates Program.

A person may initiate a claim to recover the property by filing a petition within 10 years after the death of the decedent or eight years after the entry of a decree or order of escheat. If you believe you have a claim, call the claims coordinator at (503) 986-5289 or email claim@dsl.state.or.us.

**California** also has a list of estates in a Microsoft Excel Worksheet but you have to know where to look for it. The Estates File contains names of deceased persons with the properties indexed by four categories: The State of California property ID number, the decedent's name, reported heirs and the property's available balance. You'll find the link by going to the California unclaimed property site. Scroll down and on the left is a heading "Info for Investigators." The link is under that heading.

**Arizona** allows you to claim the money within seven years of the date of the sale of the property.

My advice is to check with the probate court where your loved one died to find out what happens when heirs can't be found; or Google "Escheat Estates" and the name of your state.

**LAWYER TRUST ACCOUNTS** Lawyers holding property of clients or third persons must keep those funds separate from the lawyer's own property. Funds—including advances for costs and expenses, escrow and other funds held for another—are kept in a Lawyer Trust

Account. In Oregon, unclaimed client funds in Lawyer Trust Accounts (LTAs) and inactive Interest on Lawyer Trust Accounts (IOLTAs) at financial institutions must be remitted to the Oregon State Bar. Until claimed, the unclaimed lawyer trust and IOLTA funds paid to the bar will help fund legal services to the poor under the Legal Services Program.

The listing gets reported in name only to the state unclaimed property office, but the money is held at the Oregon State Bar. There's a lag in time between when it's deemed abandoned and when it gets reported to the state.

If your loved one had money that might have been in an LTA and you can't find it on the state unclaimed property site, check with the attorney, or the state or county bar association.

**UNPAID FOREIGN CLAIMS** The Foreign Claims Awards are certified to the Department of the Treasury for payment by the Foreign Claims Settlement Commission (FCSC), an independent quasi-judicial federal agency, which is administratively a component of the U.S. Department of Justice. The FCSC determines the validity and valuation of claims of U.S. nationals for loss of property in foreign countries, as authorized by Congress or following government-to-government settlement agreements. These losses can occur as either a result of nationalization of property by foreign governments or from damage to or loss of property as a result of military operations, or injury to both civilian and military personnel.

The Department of the Treasury's role is to ensure that the FCSC claimants receive the proper payment amount as authorized in the public law that governs each Foreign Claims Program. https://fiscal.treasury.gov/unpaid-foreign-claims/

There are listings by name for Libya, Germany, Vietnam, and War Claims.

**Libya**: https://fiscal.treasury.gov/unpaid-foreign-claims/libya-claims.html

**Germany**: https://fiscal.treasury.gov/unpaid-foreign-claims/germany-claims.html

**Vietnam**: https://fiscal.treasury.gov/unpaid-foreign-claims/vietnam-claims.html

**War Claims**: https://fiscal.treasury.gov/unpaid-foreign-claims/war-claims.html

**OIL AND MINERAL ROYALTIES** When mineral rights owners move, they rarely think to update their contact information with the clerk of the court in the county where their mineral rights are held.

The same applies when an heir inherits mineral rights. The heir needs to contact the clerk of court with their contact information and provide proof that they are the new owner.

There may be a lot of money being held for you.

For example, in 2017 Oklahoma had $73 million in unclaimed royalties held by the Oklahoma Corporation Commission that holds it for five years before turning it over to the state. Unless you know about the OCC or similar state repositories that hold the money before it gets turned over to the state, you may not be able to find your listing if you are contacted by a finder. Check with your state unclaimed property office for information they may have about where royalty money is before it goes to the state. For the Oklahoma information, go to: http://www.occeweb.com/MOEAsearch/

If you are contacted about oil or mineral royalties for a deceased relative, chances are there was an accountant involved for the purposes of filing income taxes. Look for old IRS forms and check if there is a preparer's name at the bottom of the 1040. Contact that person. You may need to provide documentation that shows you are the administrator of the estate.

John R. Thomason, an attorney in Houston Texas who is board certified in oil, gas and mineral law, said the first step is to determine who in your family may have owned it and where the property is. If you can find out what county the property is in, (everything revolves around this) check the real property records. Run indexes, check the grantee records to see if mineral or royalty rights were received and grantor records to see if they were passed on. It may be worthwhile to hire a professional Landman who is well-versed in the area (www.landman.org) is the professional organization) or an abstractor from a title company.

"You may need to go back several generations or at least for the lifetime of the ancestor," said Thomason. Also check the ad valorem property tax records.

If a company wants to drill on a property but has been unsuccessful in their attempt to locate the mineral rights owner, the company can petition the court. If the judge is satisfied with their attempts to locate the owners, a receiver is appointed. So, another avenue is to check with the clerk of the court to see if there have been any receivership actions filed. Any monies that are generated from the drilling project are held for the owners to claim.

Roger Soape, a Certified Professional Landman in Houston Texas, said "There can be a lot of research required to develop adequate ownership information to get companies to release funds to royalty owners. Usually, though, proceeds which are unclaimed or owed to unknown persons are turned over to the state where the property is located."

There are also many excellent forums on the Internet with useful information as well as people on the discussion boards who may be able to help you. One such site is www.mineralrightsforum.com. The National Association of Royalty Owners may be able to provide some direction for oil and gas royalty owners. http://www.naro-us.org

Some states have "Current Pay" rules with oil and mineral rights. This means once you have a mineral proceeds or oil royalty payment turned over to the unclaimed property office, all subsequent payments for that will be turned over even if they have not met the time criteria for escheatment.

## OLD STOCK CERTIFICATES/MINING CERTIFICATES

The Securities and Exchange Commission has a site that refers you to people who, for a fee, can help you evaluate the worth of your old certificates. Go here: https://www.sec.gov/fast-answersanswersoldcerhtm.html

Even if the company is no longer in business, they certificates may have value if that company was taken over by another. They may also have value as a collectible item. Check at https://scripophily.com for collectible value.

**POSTAL MONEY ORDERS** Lost damaged or stolen money orders can be traced here: https://www.usps.com/shop/money-orders.htm Or contact them by mail here:

Postal Data Center
Money Order Division
P.O. Box 14165
St. Louis, MO 63182-9453
(314) 436-3711

**LOST LUGGAGE** This topic and the one that follows were reader suggestions. Lost luggage goes to the Unclaimed Baggage Center in Scottsdale, Alabama. It's the largest tourist attraction in Alabama bringing 800,000 people through its doors every year. Also included are unclaimed items from bus lines, air freight and the lost and found department of airports.

The bags are opened. The items are sorted, cleaned and put up for sale. This is the part you're not going to want to hear.

You can't just go there and lay claim to your stuff. By the time it reaches the UBC, the airline has paid you for your loss. The unidentified baggage and its contents are theirs. And they ship it off to Alabama.

Here's my thought – you know that camera in your phone? Use it to take a picture of your luggage before you leave. It would be easier for the airline crew to *see* what they're looking for. Plus, if it gets damaged, you can show that it wasn't damaged when you checked it in.

Another helpful hint is that when you're headed to your destination, put the hotel or destination address on the luggage tag with your name and the dates you are staying there. Of course, you should also have your name and permanent address on the inside as well. Luggage manufacturers should include a spot inside the luggage for this purpose.

**RECOVERED STOLEN PROPERTY** Don't forget to change your address with law enforcement if you were a victim of theft in case the stolen items are recovered. It happens sometimes!

Propertyroom.com is an auction site for police and other municipal agencies that need to auction items. Some of these items were used as evidence in court trials; or recovered stolen property for which the rightful owner could not be found. You can bid on jewelry, technology, even cars and trucks.

# 20 Tips to Prevent Your Money from Going to the State

**Do these things annually!**

Preventing your money from going to the state is far easier than trying to get it back. Now that you've read this book, you're too smart to let that happen!

- Have some type of customer-initiated activity on each of your accounts. Call and verify the address that the bank has for your Certificate of Deposit, make a deposit or withdrawal on your savings account, vote your proxy on stocks, use your checking account. Every account or investment you have MUST have customer-initiated activity to prevent it from being turned over to the state. Just because you have activity on one account doesn't mean it counts toward your other accounts even within the same institution.

- Update your beneficiary information on life insurance, retirement plans etc. including their contact information. Name a secondary beneficiary in case the primary person dies.

- If your spouse or other beneficiary dies, update your beneficiary information again ASAP. Then update your will.

- Make sure your safe deposit fees are paid every year. Automatic payments are a good option. You still need customer-initiated activity on them

- Open your mail! What you may think is advertising could be a check or a notice that your money is about to be turned over to the state if you don't respond.

- When you move, know that the change of address card you fill out with the post office is only valid for one year. As mail gets forwarded to you, change the address with each company. Even if the company has Address Correction Requested on the envelope, don't assume your information is going to be updated. Don't forget to change your physical address with companies that you get e-bills from or do online banking with. There's a checklist at the end of this section to help make sure you don't miss anyone.

- Utility deposits are a common source of unclaimed property. If you've paid your electric, water or gas bill on time for a year or more, ask if the utility company will credit your deposit back to your account. Crediting your account can have an advantage over getting a check because there is no chance for a lost check.

If they say it happens automatically, ask when you can expect it and look for it. If you don't get it, follow up with them. If you don't get the refund while you are living in the residence, make sure the utility companies have your new address.

- Cash every check as soon as possible.

- Always make sure you get your final paycheck from an employer. As an example, if your last day of work is the first day of the new pay period, you will have two checks, not one. There will be one check from the pay period that just ended, plus another check from the new pay period. In addition, if you have vacation time available, some employers issue that as a separate check.

- Notify the 401K or 403B administrator and the employer sponsored insurance plans (life, health, dental) of your new address when you move. Just because you give your employer the information doesn't mean it will be shared with the others. Your benefits are your responsibility.

- If you change jobs, consider rolling your retirement plan over to your new employer or start your own IRA. That way, the account never gets lost. A rollover is not the same as a withdrawal. A withdrawal incurs penalties if you take it out before age 59 ½. A rollover usually has no penalties.

- When possible, having all your accounts in one place makes it easier to keep track of them.

- When it comes to stocks, you can't go wrong with customer-initiated activity as described above. At least once a year, call to check on the account balance, request a statement, or verify your address. Log in to your account. You can also vote your proxy. Don't rely on anyone else to do this for you. If it gets to the point that you are getting letters saying the transfer agent hasn't heard from you and your holdings might get turned over to the state unless they hear from you, then reply immediately!

- Notify everyone in the Change of Name/Address Checklist in the next section and anyone else you do business with when you have a name change. This is also an excellent tool if you are an executor of an estate.

- Make a list of your assets. Make sure someone knows where your important financial documents are in case of your death. Keep your assets and your list and location of assets in separate locations. Include items like pre-paid funeral expenses or cremation services.

- List your monthly subscriptions so they can be canceled.

- When closing out your loved one's finances at the bank, check if there was a safe deposit box.

- I have a POD designation on my checking account. This stands for Payable on Death so my family can have access immediately to cash to cover expenses.

- If your home was foreclosed, notify the Clerk of Court of an address where you can be reached in case the home sold for more than you owed. You are entitled to the amount paid in excess of your balance. The same holds true for tax liens/deeds that are sold. Make sure the property tax office has an address for you. These items are one of the few types of listings that may expire with the county keeping the funds if you don't claim them in the specified time frame.

- Your digital assets may never be found until they are turned over to the state. Your online accounts, such as PayPal, iTunes or gambling sites may have cash credits. Perhaps you have an eBay or Amazon store. Do you have an online-only bank account or other investments that never generate postal mail? Make sure your heirs have access to your login name and password so the account balances don't get escheated.

In addition, there is a wealth of online value to your digital possessions such as domain names, your irreplaceable digital photos and more. (Sometimes this is about more than just money.)

Here are a couple services that allow you to catalog all these digital treasures so your designated person has access to them after your passing:

**SecureSafe.com** is available as an app with fingerprint ID access on your smartphone. It offers a free option with up to 50 passwords. Remember to update your passwords here when you change them.

Additional levels are available where you can store important documents for a monthly fee.

This is important to know: No one at the company can see your information.

This is even more important to know: If you're using your laptop and forget your password for the site, there is no way to reset it. When you sign up, you are given a 36-character alphanumeric code you can enter if you forgot the password. You can't save the page on your computer. You have to print it and then remember where you put the paper otherwise you have to start over.

**LegacyTracker.com** was created by my Canadian counterpart, Brenda Potter Phelan, an accountant by trade. Of course, you can do the basics like enter information about your assets, including your digital assets. But you can also scan documents for storage and make a list of your household inventory including pictures. The program alerts you when items are about to expire or if something is incomplete. It will also track your net worth.

The two criteria Potter had when she created it was it had to be safe and simple. The importance of having your information available involves more than just making it easy for your loved ones after your passing. "If you're in a disaster and you lose everything, how do you begin to start over without this information?" Phelan said.

# Change of name/address or Executor of a will checklist

Use this list as a reminder of places to notify when you have a change of name or address, to list your assets for your family, or if you are the executor of an estate. In the event of a death, don't just notify the company. Change the address to the executor's home or business address. A change of address with the post office is only good for one year. This helps prevent your money from getting turned over to the state because the company lost track of you. The list is meant to be comprehensive on many levels. Not all of these involve money.

**Banking:**
Checking
Savings
Mortgage
Other loans
CD
Safe Deposit Box
Cryptocurrency (Bitcoin, etc.)

## Retirement/Investments:

Education Savings Accounts

401K

403B

IRA

Roth

Pension

Thrift Savings Plan

SEP

Mutual Funds

DRIP

Stocks

Bonds

Savings Bonds

Securities

Annuities

Trust

Retained Asset Accounts

## Insurance:

Medical/Supplemental

Mail order prescriptions/Medical Supplies

Dental

Vision

Hearing

FSA
HSA
Medicare
Whole Life
Term Life
Auto
Renters
Homeowners
Liability
Malpractice

## Professional:

Doctors
Dentist
Orthodontist
Optometrist
Mental Health
Therapy
Attorney
CPA
Hospital
Lab
Radiology
ER
Veterinarian

## Utilities:
Electric

Water

Gas

Telephone

Cell Phone

Internet

Satellite radio

Television provider

Trash pick-up

## Governmental:
Social Security Administration

Internal Revenue Service

Veterans Administration

Vehicle Registration

Local tax collector (property taxes)

State Treasurer (states with income taxes)

## Courts:
Clerk of the Court (foreclosures, tax sales, mineral rights, pending litigation)

Law enforcement (if you had stolen property in case it is recovered)

Condemnation awards
Bankruptcy
Lawsuit
Jury duty pay
Class Action lawsuit
Criminal Restitution

**Licenses**:
Driver's License/DMV
CDL
Vehicle
Boat
Airplane
Personal Watercraft
Professional (MD, RN, Cosmetology, etc.)
Home-based Business
Hunting
Fishing
Pet license

**Subscriptions:**
Newspapers
Magazines
Newsletters
AAA

AARP
Monthly subscriptions
Professional organizations

## Credit cards:
Visa
Master Card
American Express
Discover
Retail Stores
Gas

## Accounts receivable:
Employer
Payroll cards
Worker comp benefits
Child Support
Alimony
Commissions
Consulting Fees
Performance Royalties/Residuals
Oil and Mineral Royalties
    (Check suspense accounts too)
Timber Royalties

## Retail:
Layaway
Savings Clubs (Sam's, Costco, etc.)
Store loyalty cards with rewards

## Cultural:
Church
Library
School
College
Alumni Association
Sorority/Fraternity
Museums
Theatre
Botanical
Civic Organizations

## Online accounts:
PayPal
Apple Pay
Google Pay
Apps with money on them
Games (Gambling, etc.)
Online stores (Amazon, eBay, etc.)
Domain names
Frequent flier programs

**Miscellaneous:**

Storage units

Loan Collateral

Prepaid tolls

Pre-paid funeral expenses

Gambling winnings

Escrow

Earnest money

Retainer fees (Lawyers)

Pet ID tag on collar/microchip

Membership fees (gyms, clubs, etc.)

## *Fun Fact*

*In 2016 nearly $12 million of casino gambling tickets were unclaimed in Nevada.*

# State Unclaimed Property Contacts

I listen to reader feedback. One of the requests was to have the state contact information available for those who don't have computer access. Here it is.

I've included two additional items. One is how often the state site updates its information. The other is state-specific information about professional finders.

Let me tell you . . . as proficient as I am at searching online, finding this information was a real challenge. If I had to read through the state statutes, I included the number of the statute. If you want to search yourself, here's a hint based on my experience: start at the bottom and work up. For example, New Jersey's unclaimed property law is 245 pages. The information about finders is on page 240.

I don't understand why states don't provide this information front and center on their site. In some cases, there was nothing whatsoever online. Michigan would only send me a pack of info. They wouldn't just answer the question. I feel states owe their residents this kind of information.

There were some things in common among many states. Check with your own state to see if these apply:

- You can claim a fee is unconscionable.

- Some states have limitations on the fee, but if you are willing, they can be exceeded with a full disclosure form that specifies the nature of the property, who it is from, the dollar amount, and the amount you will receive after the finder's fee.

- In the case of oil or mineral royalties that are due to you, the finder cannot take a portion of your holdings, only the dollar amount that is due you.

Remember that these rules only apply to listings on the state unclaimed property sites. If you get contacted about money that is in the pre-escheat phase or money that will not get turned over to the state, you're on your own. But knowing what your state standard is may give you some bargaining room.

## Alabama
Office of the State Treasurer
Unclaimed Property Division

P.O. Box 302520
Montgomery, AL 36130-2520
(334) 242-9614
(888) 844-8400
Updated: Every several months
Finders: Contract is void if it was entered into from the date the property was presumed abandoned until 24 months after it has been in the possession of the state treasurer. 35-12-93. Newly added: 10% limit on fees.

## Alaska
State of Alaska
Treasury Division
P.O. Box 110405
Juneau, AK 99811-0405
(907) 465-3726
Updated:  As reports come in
Finders: Fees limited to 10% on property above $500; 20% on property less than $500. No requirements or licenses.

## Arizona
Department of Revenue
Unclaimed Property Unit
P.O. Box 29026

Phoenix, AZ 85038-9026

(602) 364-0380

(877) 492-9957

Updated: Every 14 days

Finders: Fee cannot exceed 30%. Must be currently licensed private investigators. Money must have been in state possession for 2 years.

## Arkansas

Auditor of State

Unclaimed Property Division

1401 W Capitol Ave, Suite 325

Little Rock, AR 72201-1811

(501) 682-6000

(800) 252-4648

Updated: Annually in the spring. Changing to a new system that will allow more frequent updates.

Finders: Maximum fee is 10%.

## California

Office of State Controller

Unclaimed Property Division

White Rock Rd., Suite 141

Rancho Cordova, CA 95670

(916) 323-2827
(800) 992-4647
Updated: Monthly
Finders: Fee not more than 10% except for County Probated Estates which have no limit.

## Colorado
Department of the Treasury
Great Colorado Payback
1580 Logan, Suite 500
Denver, CO 80203
(303) 866-6070
(800) 825-2111
Updated: As reports come in
Finders: Fee is limited to 20%. Property must be in possession of the state for at least 24 months.

## Connecticut
Office of the State Treasurer
Unclaimed Property Division
P.O. Box 5065
Hartford, CT 06102
(860) 702-3125
(800) 833-7318

Updated: As reports come in.

Finders: Fee is limited to 10%

## Delaware

Delaware Bureau of Unclaimed Property

Department of Finance

Division of Revenue

State Escheater

P.O. Box 8931

Wilmington, DE 19801-3509

(302) 577-8220

Updated: annually, end of October.

Finders: No rules

## District of Columbia

Office of Finance and Treasury

Unclaimed Property Unit

1101 4th St SW, Suite W800-B

Washington DC 20024

(202) 442-8181

Updated: Weekly

Finders: Fee limited to 10%. May exceed this if the agreement is in writing, signed by owner, specifies nature and value of property and the holder. Owner may assert at any time that the fee is excessive or unjust. Must be in possession at least 7 months. § 41-137

## Florida

Department of Financial Services
Unclaimed Property Bureau
200 East Gaines St,
Tallahassee, FL 32399-0358
(850) 413-5555
(888) 258-2253
Updated: Monthly
Finders: Fees are limited to 20% up to a max of $1,000 per account. This may be exceeded if the original contract you signed contains a full disclosure. Call for details. Must be licensed as a CPA, attorney or private investigator.

## Georgia

Georgia Department of Revenue
Unclaimed Property Section
4125 Welcome All Rd., Ste. 701
Atlanta, GA 30349
(855) 329-9863

Updated: Daily
Finders: Fee is not to exceed 10%. Listing must be in state possession for at least 24 months. §44-12-224

## Hawaii
Department of Budget and Finance
Unclaimed Property Program
P.O. Box 150
Honolulu, HI 96810
(808) 586-1589
Updated: Monthly
Finders: Fee is not to exceed 10%. Listing must be in state possession for at least 24 months. §523A-25

## Idaho
State Treasurer's Office
Unclaimed Property Program
P.O. Box 83720
Boise, ID 83720-9101
(208) 332-2942
(877) 388-2942
Updated: Annually in January
Finders: No regulations on finders or limit on fees. Listing must be in state possession at least 24 months.

## Illinois

Office of the State Treasurer

Unclaimed Property Division

P.O. Box 19495

Springfield, IL 62794-9495

(217) 785-6998

(800) 961-8303

Listings prior to 1992 and those less than $5 are not on the web site. Call to check.

Updated:  Weekly

Finders:  Fees are limited to 10%. Must be registered as detectives with the IL Dept. of Professional Regulation. Listing must be in state possession at least 24 months.


## Indiana

Office of the Attorney General

Unclaimed Property Division

P.O. Box 2504

Greenwood, IN 46142

(866) 462-5246

**25-year limit to claim**

Updated: Daily

Finders: May charge up to 10%.

## Iowa

Great Iowa Treasure Hunt
Lucas State Office Building
321 E 12th St, 1st Floor
Des Moines, IA 50319
(515) 281-5367
Updated: As reports come in
Finders: Fees are limited to 15%. Must be licensed as private investigators. Listing must be in state possession at least 24 months.

## Kansas

Kansas State Treasurer
Unclaimed Property Division
900 SW Jackson, Suite 201
Topeka, KS 66612-1235
(785) 296-3171
(800) 432-0386
Updated: Annually and as reports come in
Finders: Fee is not to exceed 15%. Listing must be in state possession at least 24 months.

## Kentucky

Kansas State Treasurer

Unclaimed Property Division

1050 US Hwy 127 South, Suite 100

Frankfort, KY 40601

(502) 564-4722

(800) 465-4722

Updated: Nightly

Finders: Fees are limited to 10%. Agreements made between the date the property was assumed abandoned and extending through 24 months after the property was delivered to the State Treasurer are void and unenforceable. 393.117

## Louisiana

Office of the State Treasurer

Unclaimed Property Division

P.O. Box 91010

Baton Rouge, LA 70821-9010

(225) 219-9400

(888) 925-4127

Updated: Almost every night

Finders: Fee is limited to 10%. Listing must be in state possession for at least 24 months.

## Maine

Office of the State Treasurer
Attn: Unclaimed Property
39 State House Station
Burton M. Cross Bldg. 3rd Floor
111 Sewall St,
Augusta, ME 04333-0039
(207) 624-7470
(888) 283-2808
Updated: Nightly
Finders: Agreements made more than 24 months and less than 36 months after the listing are presumed abandoned are limited to 15%. Must be licensed as a private investigator in Maine. §1976

## Maryland

Comptroller of Maryland
Unclaimed Property Unit
301 W. Preston St.
Baltimore, MD 21201-2385
(410) 767-1700
(800) 782-7383
**Call to have listings less than $100 searched.**
Updated: At least once a month

Finders: Listing must have been in state custody for at least 24 months.

## Massachusetts
Department of the State Treasurer
Abandoned Property Division
One Ashburton Place, 12th Floor
Boston, MA 02108-1608
(617) 367-0400
(800) 647-2300
Updated: Daily
Finders: Fees are limited to 10%. Must be registered with the Abandoned Property Division. Finders may not also represent holders doing pre-escheat work. Listing must have been on the state site for 24 months.

## Michigan
Department of the Treasury
Unclaimed Property Division
P.O. Box 30756
Lansing, MI 48909
(517) 636-5320
Updated: Monthly
Finders: No limit on fees. May need to be licensed as

a private investigator in order to lawfully conduct investigations with respect to finding owners of unclaimed property.

## Minnesota

Department of Commerce
Unclaimed Property Program
85 7th Place East, Suite 280
St. Paul, MN 55101-2198
(651) 539-1545
(800) 925-5668
Updated weekly on Tuesday
Finders: Fee is limited to 10%. This amount can be exceeded if the document you signed contains a full disclosure. Call for details. Must be registered as a private investigator. Listing must have been in state possession for 24 months.

## Mississippi

Mississippi Treasury
Unclaimed Property Division
P.O. Box 138
Jackson, MS 39205
(601) 359-3600

Updated: Nightly

Finders: Fee is limited to 10%. Treasurer reviews all contracts. Listing must be in state possession at least seven months.

## Missouri

State Treasurer's Office

Unclaimed Property Section

P.O. Box 1004

Jefferson City, MO 65102-1272

(573) 751-0840

Updated: Nightly, Monday-Friday

Finders: Property in state possession for:

- More than 12 months but less than 24 months are limited to 10%;

- More than 24 months but less than 36 months are limited to 15%;

- More than 36 months is limited to 20%.

Finders must register with the State Treasurer and certify compliance and good standing with the tax, business registration and all other regulatory requirements as required in Missouri. To remain certified, the person must annually recertify compliance with such requirements. Property must be in state possession at least 12 months. (Statute 447.581)

## Montana

Department of Revenue

Attn: Unclaimed Property

P.O. Box 5805

Helena, MT 59604-5805

(406) 444.6900

(866) 859-2254

Updated: Annually

Finders: Any fee above 15% is considered unconscionable.

## Nebraska

Office of the State Treasurer

Unclaimed Property Division

809 P St.

Lincoln, NE 68508

(402) 471-2455

(877) 572-9688

Updated: Daily

Finders: Fees are limited to 10%. Listing must have been in state possession for at least 24 months. 69-1317

## Nevada

Office of the State Treasurer
Unclaimed Property Division
555 E. Washington Ave, Suite 4200
Las Vegas, NV 89101-1070
(702) 486-4140
(800) 521-0019
Updated: Nightly
Finders: Fees are limited to 10%. May be required to be licensed as private investigator.

## New Hampshire

Treasury Department
Unclaimed Property Division
25 Capitol St. Room 205
Concord, NH 03301
(603) 271-2619
(800) 791-0920
**Processing fee of $20 for liquidation or re-registration of securities**
Updated: Monthly
Finders: Listing must be in state possession for at least 24 months.

## New Jersey

Office of the State Treasurer

Unclaimed Property Administration

P.O. Box 214

Trenton, NJ 08625-0214

(609) 292-9200

Updated: Monthly

Finders: Fee is not to exceed 20%, except if it is in the pre-escheat phase when 35% is allowed. Listing must be in state possession for at least 24 months. 46:30B-106

## New Mexico

Taxation and Revenue Department

Unclaimed Property Division

P.O. Box 25123

Santa Fe, NM 67504-5123

(505) 476-1774

Updated: Weekly

Finders: Agreement is void and unenforceable if it was entered in from the date the property was presumed abandoned until 48 months after it was received by the unclaimed property administrator. 7-8A-25 NMSA 1978

## New York

Office of the State Comptroller
Office of Unclaimed Funds
110 State Street, 8th floor
Albany, NY 12236
(518) 270-2200
(800) 221-9311
Updated: Weekly
Finders: Maximum fee is 15%
Call for listings prior to 1985 or for listings less than $20

## North Carolina

Department of State Treasurer
Unclaimed Property Office
3200 Atlantic Ave.
Raleigh, NC 27904-1668
(919) 508-1000
(800) 582-0615
Updated: Every Monday
Finders: Fee is limited to $1,000 or 20%, whichever is less. Finders must be registered and pay an annual fee. May need private investigator license. Pre-escheat agreements are void and unenforceable. Must be in state possession for 24 months.

## North Dakota

North Dakota Dept. of Trust Lands
Unclaimed Property Division
P.O. Box 5523
Bismarck, ND 58506-5523
(701) 328-2800
Updated: As reports are received
Finders: Fee is not to exceed 10%. Must be licensed as a private investigator. Listing must be in state possession for at least 24 months.

## Ohio

Department of Commerce
Division of Unclaimed Funds
77 S. High St., 20th Floor
Columbus, OH 43215-6108
(877) 644-6823
Updated: Weekly
Finders: Fee is limited to 10%. Finders must have a Certificate of Registration. Listing must be in state possession for at least 24 months.

## Oklahoma

Office of the State Treasurer-UPD

State Capitol Building

2300 N. Lincoln, Room 217

Oklahoma City, OK 73105

(405) 521-4273

Updated: Daily

Finders: Fee is limited to 25%

## Oregon

Department of State Lands

Unclaimed Property Section

775 Summer St. NE, Suite 100

Salem, OR 97301-1279

(503) 986-5200 ext. 65293#

Updated: Daily, Monday-Friday

Finders: Must be licensed as a private investigator. Information on unclaimed property accounts is confidential for 1 year prior to going to the state and for 2 years once it's been turned over to the state.

## Pennsylvania

Pennsylvania Treasury

P.O. Box 1837

Harrisburg, PA 17105-1837

(717) 787-2465

(800) 222-2046

**Newspaper publication does not have to include listings less than $250.**

Updated: "Often"

Finders: Fees are limited to 15%. § 1301.11 (g)


## Rhode Island

P.O. Box 1435

Providence, RI 02901

(401) 462-7676

Updated: Weekly

Finders: Must be in state possession at least 24 months. § 33-21.1-35


## South Carolina

State Treasurer's Office

Unclaimed Property Program

P.O. Box 11778

Columbia, SC 29211

(803) 737-4771

**Some listings go back to the 1940s**

Updated: Weekly

Finders: Fees are limited to 15%. Family Privacy Protection Act forbids information obtained from the state agencies to be used for commercial purposes. Listing must be with the state for at least 24 months.

**South Dakota**

Office of the State Treasurer

Unclaimed Property Division

500 E. Capitol Ave., Suite 212

Pierre, SD 57501-5070

(605) 773-3379

(866) 357-2547

Updated: Weekly

Finders: Fees are limited to 25% unless you agree in writing to pay more. Agreements made between 1 year prior to going to the state and for 2 years once it's been turned over to the state are unenforceable. 43-41B-36

**Tennessee**

Treasury Department

Unclaimed Property Division

502 Deaderick St.

Nashville, TN 37243-0203

(615) 741-6499

Updated: Annually

Finders: Fees are limited to 10% or $50, whichever is greater. Must be licensed as a private investigator. Signed contracts must be approved by the unclaimed property division.

## Texas

Texas Comptroller of Public Accounts

Unclaimed Property Claims Section

P.O. Box 12019

Austin, TX 78711-2019

(512) 463-3120

(800) 654-FIND (3463)

Updated: Nightly, except Saturday

Finders: Fees are limited to 10%. Must be licensed through the Texas Dept. of Public Safety, Private Security Bureau and hold a current sales tax permit.

## Utah

State Treasurer's Office

Unclaimed Property Division

P.O. Box 140530

Salt Lake City, UT 84114

(801) 715-3300

(888) 217-1203

Updated: Daily

Finders: Listing must be in state possession for at least 24 months. 67-4a-705


## Vermont

Office of the State Treasurer

Unclaimed Property Division

109 State St. 4th Floor

Montpelier, VT 05609-6200

(802) 828-2407

(800) 642-3191 (VT only)

TTY (800) 253-0191

Updated: Daily

Finders: Fee is limited to 10%. Must register with the Treasurer's office and post a $10,000 bond. Listing must be in state possession for at least 24 months. § 1265


## Virginia

Virginia Dept. of the Treasury

Division of Unclaimed Property

P.O. Box 2478
Richmond, VA 23218-2478
(804) 225-2393
(800) 468-1088
Updated: Weekly
Finders: Fee is limited to 10%. Must have a valid business license in Virginia. Listing must be in state possession for 36 months.

## Washington
Department of Revenue
Unclaimed Property Section
P.O. Box 47477
Olympia, WA 98504-7477
(360) 705-6706
(800) 435-2429 (WA only)
Updated: As reports come in
Finders: Fee is limited to 5% and that's not just the state unclaimed property site. It includes 5 % for finding listings in cities, counties and other municipalities in regard to foreclosure proceeds. Finders must be registered with the state.

## West Virginia

West Virginia State Treasurer's Office
Unclaimed Property Division
322 70th St. SE
Charleston, WV 25304
(304) 558-2937
(800) 642-8687
Updated: Daily
Finders: Finders are not addressed in the WV Unclaimed
Property Act.

## Wisconsin

Office of the State Treasurer
Unclaimed Property Section
P.O. Box 8982
Madison, WI 53708-8982
(608) 267-7977
(877) 699-9211
Updated: Nightly
Finders: Fees are limited to 20%. Must be in state
possession at least 12 months. Statute 177.35

## Wyoming

Wyoming Unclaimed Property
2515 Warren Ave, Suite 502
Cheyenne, WY 82002
(307) 777-5590
Call if you want a "complete" search
Updated: Monthly
Finders: Agreements made between 1 year prior to going to the state and for 2 years once it's been turned over to the state are unenforceable. 34-24-136

## US TERRITORIES

## American Samoa

Department of the Treasury
Executive Office Building
Pago Pago, AS 96799
(684) 633-4155

## Guam

Treasurer of Guam
P.O. Box 884
Hagatna, GU 96932

## Puerto Rico

Office of the Commissioner of Financial Institutions
Unclaimed Property
P.O. Box 11855
San Juan, PR 00910-3855
(787) 723-3131 ext 2354

## Virgin Islands

Office of the L Governor
Division of Banking
#18 Kongens Gade
St. Thomas, Virgin Islands 00802
(340) 774-7166

## CANADA

## Alberta

Tax and Revenue Administration
Alberta Treasury Board and Finance
9811 109 St.
Edmonton, AB T5K 2L5
(780) 427-3044

## British Columbia

British Columbia Unclaimed Property Society

Box 18519

West Georgia RPO

Vancouver, BC V6Z 0B3

(604) 662-3518

(888) 662-2877

**They have listings back to the late 1800s!**

## Bank of Canada

Unclaimed Balance Services

234 Wellington St.

Ottawa, ON K1A 0G9

(800) 303-1282

## Quebec

Direction principale des biens non réclamés

Revenu Québec

500, boulevard René-Lévesque Ouest, bureau 10.00

Montréal, Québec QC H2Z 1W7

(866) 840-6939 – (800) 361-3795 Hearing Impaired

# Afterword

I hope you have found this information useful. I truly hope this helps you find your money. I welcome your comments or additional information I may not have included or topics I didn't cover.

With this 4th edition, my thanks go to my same core group of supporters: my mom, my son Ryan, my daughter-in-law Kelly; Vicki Bottorf, who first told me about the missing money sites; Linda Ulrich for her inspiration; Dr. Frazier for his generous support in my idea and my ability to achieve it as well as his financial support, plus his referral of Carol Bassett—my Editor (Thank you, Carol!); Steven Salyer who personifies integrity and unflappable commitment to get the job done; Peter Preovolos, you're amazing! You get it. You completely understand what I'm doing. Thank you so much for your support!

I especially want to thank all the media outlets that have been so gracious about letting me share this information with folks. I never know when someone has been praying for a financial miracle. They hear this information. Check it out. And their life is transformed.

My goal is to make my book obsolete by making sure people know how to prevent their money from going to the state in the first place. I also want to give them every opportunity to find their money on their own and not have to pay someone for it. It's the "give a man a fish, feed him for a day; teach a man to fish, feed him for a lifetime," school of thought.

Finding missing money isn't a one-time thing. People need to check at least once a year.

I've been told my business model is wrong—I should be charging people for finding their money. It's true that I'd be making a whole lot more than what I'm doing with the book. But I don't think people should have to pay a ransom to get their own money.

I believe that if I hold true to what I believe in my heart is the right thing to do, that it will come back to me. I can't do this any other way.

Happy treasure hunting!

*Mary Pitman*

# Can this information benefit your customers?

Book Mary Pitman to speak at your next event. She will customize her presentation for any audience. She can not only help the attendees find money for themselves, but also for the businesses they represent.
Call (772) 501-3941 for more information.

Would you like your company logo on the cover of
*The Little Book of Missing Money?*
Bulk sales and/or licensing options are available with or without the custom cover. Your company will make a lasting impression when your customers, clients or employees find money they didn't even know they were missing!
Email marycpitman@gmail.com with your needs.

Book Mary Pitman for your event
*and*
order the book in bulk for the best rates!
Call (772) 501-3941